SIR JOHN EDWIN SANDYS

1844–1922

SIR JOHN EDWIN SANDYS

1844-1922

by

N. G. L. HAMMOND, M.A.

*Formerly Scholar of Gonville and Caius College, Cambridge, and
Sandys Student. Fellow of Clare College, Cambridge*

CAMBRIDGE

AT THE UNIVERSITY PRESS

1933

CAMBRIDGE UNIVERSITY PRESS
Cambridge, New York, Melbourne, Madrid, Cape Town,
Singapore, São Paulo, Delhi, Mexico City

Cambridge University Press
The Edinburgh Building, Cambridge CB2 8RU, UK

Published in the United States of America by Cambridge University Press, New York

www.cambridge.org
Information on this title: www.cambridge.org/9781107681637

© Cambridge University Press 1933

First published 1933
First paperback edition 2013

A catalogue record for this publication is available from the British Library

ISBN 978-1-107-68163-7 Paperback

TO

LADY M. G. SANDYS

in grateful acknowledgment of
courteous assistance

CONTENTS

CONTENTS

CHAPTER I

1844 1867

JOHN EDWIN SANDYS was born on May 19, 1844, at Leicester, to the Rev. Timothy Sandys and his wife Rebecca: the early years of his life, from the ages of one and a half to eleven, were spent at Calcutta. Apart from the fact that the grandfather of Timothy Sandys was Isaac Sandys, of Prescot, Lancashire, a member of the Society of Friends, who was born about 1720, little is known of the immediate ancestry of the Sandys family; this is probably in part due to the father of Timothy Sandys being renounced by his family for attending a race-meeting at Doncaster, and later refusing to introduce his family to his relatives. It is, however, possible that Isaac Sandys was a member of the principal Sandys family, which was for many generations resident in Lancashire and traced its descent from the twelfth century; an interesting family epitaph may be seen in Hawkshead church, Lancashire, dedicated in memory of William and Margaret Sandys, the parents of Edwin Sandys, of St John's College, Cambridge (1519–88), Master of Catharine Hall, Bishop of Worcester and London, and Archbishop of York. This epitaph was translated in 1894 by John Edwin Sandys, whose own career was not unlike that of his namesake:

Great were the pledges of favour divine they received in abundance;
Greatest of all was the fame won them by Edwin their son.
Doctor was he, and Proctor, and Head of a College at Cambridge:
Thrice as a Bishop enthroned, thrice was he head of a See.

The property of the principal Sandys family was Gray-thwaite Hall, situated on the shores of Lake Windermere.

Timothy Sandys, the father of John Edwin, devoted his life from the age of twenty-six to missionary work in India; he was an impetuous and untiring worker in all departments of the missionary field, of whom it was written after his death: "He preached in the bazaars and taught in the schools; itinerated in villages and visited the upper classes at their homes; catechised inquirers and taught his teachers; and the result was that scarcely any man in the capital of India could thank God for so large a number of spiritual children". Doubtless the industry and the ungrudging devotion to duty of John Edwin in his later career was partly inspired by the early associations of his family life: he too was of a deeply religious nature, as is shown by his early ambition to be a missionary and by the regularity of his religious observance throughout his life. The influence of their father's example is also seen in the lives of the three elder brothers of John Edwin: the eldest as a Government clerk died of fever in Calcutta, the second as a missionary student was killed on the first day of the Indian Mutiny, the third took Holy Orders and spent many years of service in India. The closest of the family in age, as in affection, to John Edwin was his sister Priscilla, two years his senior, who married the Rev. R. R. Winter, of the Delhi Mission; but, owing to the conditions of Indian life, his boyhood was lonely, for while he was in India the older children were being educated in England. In 1853, when John Edwin was nine, his mother died of cholera, and in the following year his father married his second wife, Emily Guthrie Stuart, by whom he had two sons and two daughters: of these two subsequently undertook missionary work.

The first school attended by John Edwin was a day-school in Calcutta: while journeying to this school in a dogcart an accident befell him, which affected his health for life and prevented him from taking strenuous exercise. During his childhood he also learnt to speak both Hindustani and Bengali, and knew several Oriental alphabets. In later life he retained his interest in India, following and supporting the activities of the Delhi Mission, and preserving a little of his knowledge of Oriental languages: this interest is recorded by J. S. Reid in a short obituary notice published in the *Proceedings of the British Academy*:

When a Professorship of Sanskrit was established and the late Professor Cowell ("sanctum et venerabile nomen") was appointed to be the first holder, his earliest course of lectures was given on Comparative Philology to four listeners, of whom Mrs Cowell was one, while the other three were Sir Frederick Pollock, Sir John Sandys and myself.... A little later, Professor Cowell (whose enthusiasm for teaching was remarkable) read Sanskrit with a small class, consisting of Sandys, the late Professor Skeat, the late Charles Walter Moule, and myself.

In 1855, at the age of eleven, he was sent home to England, sailing round the Cape of Good Hope under the careful escort of two German missionaries, who taught him to play chess. In England he resided at the Church Missionary Children's Home, Islington, London, where he was educated for the following four years. Soon after his arrival in England he received the following letter from his father:

1-2

My dear John Edwin,

Your journal reached us last evening from which we were happy to learn that you had had a pleasant voyage, and had reached London in health and safety. The Ansorges appear to have done all for you that we could desire and your fellow passengers and the Captain appear to have been kind and agreeable people. I suppose by this time you have got settled in the C.M. Children's Home....I desire to bless and praise our Heavenly Father for his goodness in having preserved you during the voyage and permitted you to reach England in good health, and I hope and trust that the divine blessing may rest upon you in all your future course, that you may be a pious, diligent and attentive pupil and make such advancement in Scriptural and Scientific and useful knowledge as may with God's blessing qualify you to become a useful man when you shall have grown up. You have hitherto taken pleasure in your studies, and this I trust will continue to be the case, for such students as delight in their studies advance with much greater ease, and make much more efficient advancement than such as take no delight or feel no pleasure in their duties. You can let us know what studies you have been set to, and what you think of the advantages of education in England over those you have enjoyed in Calcutta. You will find it of advantage to take suitable and sufficient bodily exercise which will tend to giving you a strong and healthy constitution....

> With our best love I remain, my dear John Edwin,
> your very affectionate father

> T. SANDYS.

He was still at the Church Missionary Children's Home when the Indian Mutiny broke out; the first victim of the rising at Delhi on May 11, 1857 was his elder brother Daniel Corrie Sandys, then a missionary student of twenty-two years of age. A letter to John

Edwin from his sister Priscilla describes the circumstances of his death:

> We are now quite settled at Delhi, a place full of memories of dear Daniel. The natives here confirm the report that as soon as he heard the Mutiny had taken place he said to his Moonshi, who was at his house at the time: "I will just go and take this boy (the brother of his fiancée) to his parents and return quickly". But he never came back as a party of Sepoys met him on his way home and shot him in his buggy.

The courageous and untimely end of his elder brother always remained a vivid memory and a shining example to John Edwin, and it probably strengthened his inclination to devote his life also to the missionary field. His remaining years at the Missionary Home were overshadowed by the dangerous circumstances in which his family was placed by the Indian Mutiny.

In 1859, as he had rapidly outgrown the teaching of the Missionary Home, he was sent to Repton School, an old foundation which, after a period of decline, had begun to revive under the able headmastership of the Rev. S. A. Pears, D.D., sometime Fellow of Corpus, Oxford. He entered the house of the Rev. Edward Latham, whose father had preceded Mr Sandys at the Calcutta Mission and was a friend of the Sandys family. In later years Sandys often remembered with gratitude and affection the assistance afforded to him in the early period of his school career by his headmaster and his housemaster. On attending the three hundred and fiftieth anniversary of the foundation of Repton, Dr Sandys recalled the memories of his early life at school, describing himself as "a studious boy" and "a boy given to books": but if books claimed much of his attention, he was even at an early age keenly interested in most things which came within the orbit of his experience. When he was told that he would go to Repton, he did not even know where it was, "but", he says, "I seized the largest gazetteer that I could find, and had soon mastered all the antiquarian details as to the ancient seat and burial place of the bygone Mercian Kings". While he was at Repton, his health was not robust, but, despite the effects of his accident in Calcutta, he participated in the school routine of games; later he looked back with gratitude to the compulsory football which had developed his strength. After leaving Repton for the freer air of Cambridge, he had little time for games; he appears, however, in a Cambridge letter to *The Reptonian* as coxing the winning O.R. four in a race, where coxing was evidently important.

The only event in the aquatic line which will prove of any interest to Reptonians, as such, is the Repton "Scratch Fours". These races came off on December 2nd, 1865. The boats that entered were five in number, implying the existence of at least twenty-five Reptonians at Cambridge. The upsetting of one of the boats behind that which was eventually victorious, gave additional liveliness to the scene from the banks.

At Repton his ability as a scholar and the soundness of his character were early recognised: the first report sent to his father was highly laudatory, to judge from his father's letter to John Edwin:

My dear John Edwin,   *8th August* 1859. *Calcutta.*
    I am happy to learn that you are now settled at Repton....
I was glad to read the report Mr Latham had sent to Mr Stuart

concerning you, and I sincerely hope that you have continued to justify the good opinion he then had of you. It is our sincere hope that with God's blessing upon the instruction which you now receive you may become qualified for usefulness when you shall have grown up, if it should please God to spare you until you shall have done so.

With our united love
I remain
Your very affectionate father

T. SANDYS.

In 1861 he reached the Sixth Form and gained three prizes; he also began to develop in character, a fact noticed by his housemaster, who hoped that Sandys was destined for work in the missionary field.

My dear Mr Sandys,   *October* 18, 1862. *Repton*

Your son is doing very well here, and I trust that the grace of God is indeed working in his heart. His conduct and diligence are exemplary, and he seems possessed of abilities which will at this rate secure him a somewhat distinguished career at Cambridge, and what is far more, will fit him to aid the promotion of Christ's kingdom (humanly speaking) largely. It is a great pleasure to see such boys as he and Thomas and Frost are turning out—proofs that those who for the kingdom of God's sake have withdrawn from their sons some of the ordinary benefits of a home and paternal education, do not really cause their sons loss, for God becomes more than ever their Father.

Edwin does not at present seem inclined to foreign work I think; he rather looks forward to going through the University and taking orders in England. This is the best training for a missionary I fancy: which I cannot help in my heart of hearts hoping that he will ultimately become. For the claims are so great and the work so noble and the men so obviously blest of God, that it is the best I could wish for my dearest friends. Still that it should be spontaneous is the first requirement. And such a clergyman as Edwin promises to make, if God's blessing follows him in the same course as hitherto, is beyond price in old England.

He is thin, but strong and apparently quite healthy, a different person altogether from what he was when first he came here. And there is a freshness and sincerity of mind and manner, with a quiet manly reserve and modesty, which is very pleasing. He is rather deficient in general interests and still almost too quiet, but it is a fault on the right side, and he has much opened out since he became Sixth form. You see I write freely to a father who has not seen his boy for many years, what I think will interest him....

Sincerely wishing you a continual blessing in your labours and in your family—in Edwin not least I am sure—I beg to remain,

My dear Sir,

yours very faithfully,

E. LATHAM.

At this time, when his intellect and interests were expanding, he formed many close and lasting friendships, born during the country walks which he took on Sundays with chosen companions. Two of these friends he retained throughout his life, Will Bagshawe, later headmaster of the lower school at Uppingham (at whose home in Derbyshire Sandys spent many of his school holidays), and W. F. A. Archibald, later Master of the Supreme Court of Judicature; in his choice of friends is reflected his own character, for the former of these two writes in the term after Sandys left Repton: "I will say that I hate the rifle corps fearfully, only as the Doctor wishes it I think we ought not to care for a little trouble, but try and keep it up well for the credit of the school". During his last year at Repton Sandys was head-boy of Latham's house, and was succeeded in that

8

position by Will Bagshawe in 1863-4. Of his other contemporaries at Repton we may mention two. One was his "almost namesake", that distinguished scholar, Professor Sanday, in whose school study Sandys used to read portions of the classical authors. More than forty years after the school association of the two had ceased, Sandys, as Public Orator, in presenting Sanday for an Honorary Degree spoke of him as "condiscipulus", and said that he himself was "non immemor actae non alio rege puertiae". Another contemporary was H. E. Fanshawe, subsequently Fellow Classical Lecturer and Tutor of Corpus Christi College, Cambridge.

It had been decided that Sandys should go to Cambridge, and Dr Pears in a letter to Mr Sandys warmly recommended St John's College, and expressed the high hopes he entertained for John Edwin in a University career. He writes in 1862:

Your son continues to be a most satisfactory pupil, very attentive and gradually unfolding considerable mental power. There is every prospect, if his life and health last, of his gaining high distinction at the University; and at St John's College, I have little doubt, he will receive substantial encouragement —I have known young men of like character receive so much assistance in that College, as to pay their own way through College life from first to last.

Of his personal character Mr Latham knows more than I.

I have a strong impression that he is a boy of sound and deeply seated religious conviction and feeling. I believe he leaves the question of future employment still open, in which I think him right, with a strong leaning to the ministry, either at home or abroad....Let me add that it will give my wife and me a sincere pleasure to receive Mrs Sandys, whenever she is disposed to come to Repton.

9

In the spring of 1863 he gained a minor scholarship at St John's College, Cambridge, and he went into residence in the following October. He ended his career at Repton in a blaze of glory by winning six school prizes, four for Classical Composition and two for English Essay and English Verse. As his father was a man of limited means, Sandys lived almost entirely on his scholarships during his residence in Cambridge, but thanks to the generosity of St John's College and Repton School he appears to have suffered no severe financial disabilities. At St John's College he was greatly helped by the Tutor, Mr Hadley, a man in whom Dr Pears placed the highest confidence. The Master of St John's College at this time was Dr Bateson, a man of wide interests and a leading figure in University politics; he was largely responsible for the new Statutes of 1860, which replaced those dating from the reign of Henry VIII. Nor was he solely an able administrator; during the years of his mastership (1857–81) St John's College enjoyed a period of great prosperity: in his time the new College chapel first proposed in 1687 was built, and the College library was extended. We read of him in the *College History*: "'As Master of the college', said one who was intimately acquainted with him, 'Dr Bateson was ever ready to take the lead in widening and increasing the teaching powers of the college, and in rewarding intellectual distinction of every kind'". Under such a Master Sandys passed his undergraduate days, was elected Fellow of St John's College and held the office of College Tutor.

Apart from his academic successes there is little to

record of Sandys' undergraduate life; he fostered the friendships which he had contracted at Repton, and formed others on the Sunday walks which he was in the habit of taking. He spent one vacation each year at the home of his school friend, W. F. A. Archibald, in Kent. Otherwise he appears to have applied himself with characteristic energy to the business of the present, distinction as a classical scholar. In his first year he won the senior Bell Scholarship, and in his second year the Browne Medal for Greek Ode and the Porson Prize for Greek Verse Composition. In the following year he was again Porson Prizeman and also Members' Prizeman for a Latin Essay on the subject "Abraham Lincoln". These successes were a source of great joy to his parents and to the staff at Repton. Writing in 1866 Dr Pears says:

I am so truly glad of your success again. I should fear for some men this kind of honour, so great and so unusual, is exciting and intoxicating, but I have watched with sincere pleasure its effects on you hitherto, and I do not think it has done any mischief hitherto.

But it gives you a noble start in life: I hope you will use it wisely, and choose a course which may make your life most useful to others—I think it will be a very happy one to yourself.

As was generally the case at that time with men who were hoping to take a high place in the Classical Tripos, Sandys was a pupil of that famous coach, Richard Shilleto, whose exact and exacting scholarship produced a long line of distinguished scholars: on the occasion of Sandys winning the Porson Prize for the second time, Richard Shilleto wrote:

My dear Sandys,   17 *May* 1866.

   I congratulate you on your success, ἕκατι ποδῶν εὐωνύμων δὶς δυοῖν.

   I am not in the best of humours, for I have gout blindness deafness and all manner of complications of maladies. However (though the English is tremendous) you have successfully tackled with it. I have put on the other page one or two suggestions.

Yours very truly,

RICHARD SHILLETO.

   I have had this—not very recently—translated "on account of two pairs of left feet".

In 1867 he was again Members' Prizeman for Latin Essay, and set the crown on his classical career by being placed Senior Classic in the Tripos of that year. The second place in the First Class was taken by Sir Frederick Pollock, and the third by Sir Sidney Colvin, later Slade Professor of Fine Art; in the same First Class was H. M. Gwatkin, also a member of St John's College, and afterwards first Dixie Professor of Ecclesiastical History, and in the same Tripos list was the name of Palmer, also of St John's College, the famous Arabic scholar and traveller. His success was well deserved: he had worked with unflagging enthusiasm and industry to fulfil the hopes and ambitions of his parents, his teachers and himself. And yet he had not shut himself away in the privacy of his study and divorced himself from undergraduate society. So warmly was he received by his fellows, when he took his degree, that *The Times* made a special comment on it. The Congregation was an exceptionally rowdy one even for those days.

The appearance of the Vice-Chancellor at two o'clock was the signal for a prolonged howl and for every kind of disapprobation. No attempt to suppress the noise could have been made with any reasonable prospect of success, and things were allowed to take their course, though probably a college Tutor "spotted" one of his pupils here and there making himself particularly obnoxious. We are not going to attempt any description of the yells and row generally....In our notice of all that was disagreeable and offensive, we ought not to omit to mention the more pleasing fact that all present joined heartily in giving the Senior Classic a warm cheer when he took his degree.

At Repton his name was added to those of the two former Senior Classics educated at that school, George Denman, then Fellow of Trinity College, and at one time a pupil of Dr Bateson, and John Peile, Master of Christ's College, Cambridge. When the news of the Tripos results reached Repton, as a school friend of Sandys wrote, "the Doctor actually galloped for joy". On this occasion Dr Pears himself wrote as follows:

My dear Sandys   *April* 3 1867.

The news we have been hoping for is just come—and the bells are ringing—and its a half-holiday—and I need hardly add you have diffused a great joy over our little community by your splendid triumph. You have been rowing a "stern race" all the way, and whether you had won or lost, I should always have greatly admired the resolution, with which you have pursued your way from first to last. To have collared and beaten so redoubtable a champion at the very end of the course is an ample reward—and we bask in the light of your success.

You will hear from others no doubt, but you will take my few words as the expression of the universal feeling here,

ever yours most truly,

S. A. PEARS.

From his housemaster he received the following letter:

My dear Fellow,   *Wednesday, Repton.*

A telegram would have conveyed a word of heartfelt congratulation to you this evening. I cannot tell you how thankful I feel for the seal set upon the soundness and thoroughness of your past labours. God has recognised and blessed you in them, and to him I know you purpose in some way or other to dedicate them. Your present rather slippery path will be like all else a training and experience to help you at some future time.

We got the telegram about you at two-thirty p.m. and were quite unequal to the ordinary labours of school, so a preliminary halfholiday was granted. They are swinging the bells now for a good peal in your honour. I have to go over and preach at Barton tonight, and don't feel toned down to the Lent sermon level at all. How glad all Reptonians and especially our house will be.

Mrs Latham begs me to send all sorts of kind and congratulatory messages—she is as heartily glad as any of us....I cannot half tell you the joy I feel.

Ever yours affectionately

E. LATHAM.

Towards his coach, Mr Shilleto, he was always grateful; and the following letter shows the warmth with which that gratitude was expressed.

                                                    1 *Scroope Terrace*
                                                     April 9 1867
My dear Sandys,

I know not how to thank you for the beautiful book— indeed I do love Montrose and Dundee, and am pleased you remembered it—and the most kind note which accompanied it. I try to do my duty to my pupils—I am not conscious of attempting to do more. The many notes which I have received this year and in former years attest that I am considered not to fail in

14

what I try to do. Yours will be among many highly-prized κειμήλια.

Thanking you very much for your costly present and your equally τίμιον δῶρον your letter,

Believe me always

very truly yours

RICHARD SHILLETO.

It is abundantly clear that his success at Cambridge had not affected the modesty and quiet reserve which were inherent in his character. And in completing his career at the University he carried away not only the memories of his scholastic achievements, but also the warm-hearted affections of many life-long friends. If we may quote from the memoir written by J. S. Reid:

> Sandys was two years my senior in University standing. I made his acquaintance almost immediately on beginning residence, and formed a friendship with him which lasted uninterruptedly until the day of his death. That friendship has counted for much in my life, and I hope that it counted for something in his. Two close associates of ours from this remote time were Professor A. S. Wilkins and E. S. Shuckburgh.

After the Classical Tripos, Sandys went for a walking tour with his elder brother in Norfolk from Cromer to Hunstanton, and they must have discussed the careers which lay open to him as Senior Classic. All the influence of his home life, the missionary zeal of his father and the example set by his elder brothers had directed his thoughts towards the ministry, whether at home or abroad; and it is clear that his headmaster and his housemaster had fostered that instinct and developed that tradition, none the less surely because they had not forced their opinions on him nor impeded his right of choice. On the other hand, years of study had bred in him a love of the classics and a belief in their educational value, two admirable qualifications for a life devoted to teaching and research; and his position as Senior Classic made it certain that he would be offered a Fellowship soon.

Whether he chose the Church or the University, his early life had already cast the mould of his character. He was exact and thorough; he was ambitious, in the sense that whatever task he undertook he would perform to the utmost limit of his ability. The ideals which had been implanted in him by his Christian upbringing and nurtured by the springs of his own religious feeling were coupled with a clarity of thought and sanity of judgment which lent a rational colouring to his emotions and prevented any extravagant ebullition of sentiment. By nature he was modest and reserved, nor did his success disturb the balance of his temperament; in later life he possessed the dignity of a man endowed with an acute sense of honour and he was always prompt in the execution of what he held to be his duty. Thus with the close of his undergraduate life the main lines of his nature were established. He had already formed the deep affections which were destined to guide his career, his love for Repton and for St John's College, and his interest in classical scholarship. When we consider the strength of his character and the scene in which his later life was laid, we can understand the words of J. S. Reid, a friend who knew him intimately from his undergraduate days to the day of his death, when he writes after the death of John Edwin Sandys:

Sandys, as I look back on his early days, appears to me as having changed very little in advancing life. There was always about him a seriousness, and I think that I may say a dignity, which seemed to me to spring from sources like those which affected the old scholars of the Renaissance, who were deeply impressed by the importance and the honourableness of the scholar's career.

CHAPTER II

1867   1875

IN the autumn of 1867 Sandys returned to Cambridge, which was destined to be the scene of a long life of devotion to classical scholarship and of service to St John's College and to the University. The probity of his character and the consciousness of duty, which had earlier turned his thoughts toward the Church, henceforth found expression in the field to which his talents as a scholar and his temperament as a man were more suitably adapted.

A few months after the Classical Tripos he was appointed Classical Lecturer at Jesus College and also at St John's College, and a few weeks later he was elected into a Fellowship at St John's College. Among the courses of lectures which he delivered during this year may be noted a course on the *Rhetoric* of Aristotle; for it was to the study of Greek and Roman oratory that he was in his early years and indeed throughout his life especially attracted. In the summer of 1868 he edited his first work, the *Ad Demonicum et Panegyricus* of Isocrates, an author who was at that time but little read. In dedicating the first-fruits of his scholarship to the Headmaster of Repton he gracefully acknowledged a debt of gratitude, to which he often referred. Dr Pears fully appreciated the compliment in a letter to Sandys:

My dear Sandys,   *October 10, 1868. Repton, Burton on Trent.*

I really feel very much pleased and flattered by your kind thought of me, and I cannot think of making any objection to your proposal.

It surely will not do any harm to your work to be marked with the name of one who has no reputation as a scholar; and it will be an instance of kindly regard which will be felt and appreciated.

This is the way in which I may hope to edge myself into a niche of fame, as the person to whom your first work was inscribed. I am glad to think that Isocrates is to be known and read again. In reading Demosthenes the other day I was struck by seeing that neither Lord Brougham nor Whiston seemed to remember that he was the "old man eloquent" of Milton's sonnet.

Believe me

yours most truly

S. A. PEARS.

The publication of Isocrates, *Ad Demonicum et Panegyricus*, was warmly received. Although only one year had elapsed since Sandys had taken his degree, and during that year most of his time had been devoted to lecturing and to coaching, the charge was not laid against him of plunging prematurely into print. The general tone of the reviews passed on this book is shown by the following, from *The Saturday Review*:

The feeling uppermost in our minds, after a careful and interesting study of this edition, is one of satisfaction and admiration; satisfaction that a somewhat unfamiliar author has been made so thoroughly readable, and admiration of the comparatively young scholar who has brought about this result by combining in the task such industry, research, and acumen as are not always found united in editors who have had decades upon decades of mature experience.

The book was primarily intended for students at the schools and at the universities, and its popularity was attested by the printing of a second edition in 1872.

While Sandys was at Repton, he acquired a taste for modern history, for which he was afterwards very grateful. Thus as long as his health permitted he took full advantage of the vacations to travel abroad, and develop his knowledge of that subject by visiting places of historical interest. Church architecture and painting he also studied with keen appreciation. His first tour abroad was undertaken in the long vacation of 1869 in the company of Mr Macmeikan of St John's College, Cambridge: they visited Paris, Lucerne and the Rhone glacier. The diary, written by Sandys during the tour, abounds in descriptions of the scenery, the churches, their travelling acquaintances—in fact of everything in which his observant nature delighted. While they were staying near the Rhone glacier, they climbed many of the surrounding mountains, and on returning from one of the Furka summits Sandys narrowly escaped a serious accident in attempting a glissade. He describes the adventure in his journal:

At last we reached a steep snow-slope, which I intended to manage by sitting down and sliding along it: but I had hardly got ready for this feat when I found myself gliding down faster than I had expected, lost hold of my alpenstock and rushed down along a curve, avoiding a rocky buttress, fell forward on to my face, lost my cap and slipped down rapidly with my head downwards unable to stop myself. Meanwhile Macmeikan, who had got down more easily by the route that he had chosen and had crossed the line of the direction of my fall, saw me falling from my position on the right and, with great presence of mind, rushed down along the snow, and threw himself into the path of my descent and thus arrested me half way down a long slope of snow terminated by a bristling line of fallen rocks, which, had I reached them, might have at the very least caused me serious injury. After this providential escape we passed slowly down the rest of the snow-slope and at last reached the margin of the glacier, which we began to cross and thus had our first experience of a succession of real crevasses: the jumping that I accomplished under the inspiration of a good example and in some cases an imperative necessity, were to myself not a little surprising; after enjoying many glimpses of the rich and deepening blue of the crevasses, we found ourselves compelled to retreat under a darkening sky, lit up in the distance by strange gleams of sunset.

His descriptions are often flavoured with the salt of a quiet humour: "on the traditional spot of the apple-exploit we saw the colossal statue of Tell—in plaster". Or his description of the baths at Leuk.

We first entered the bains pour les pauvres, where we found a number of half-boiled and flabby forms of humanity lunging to and fro in the water. Then to several other more elaborate bathhouses: the patients stay for almost four hours up to their necks in water, clothed in dark bathing gowns with wooden floats to rest upon; at one of the tanks a fairy island of bright flowers was floating, like Delos, on the waters; at another we found a pair of very thoughtful chess-players: at another a family party playing at dominoes; elsewhere a newspaper was being read. In one or two of the baths, the bathers were vigorously carrying out the precepts of Fabricius "in balneis hilarem esse oportet", by splashing one another and indulging either in loud laughter or in animated and excited recitations.

After parting with Macmeikan, who was returning to England, Sandys was joined by his friend Mr Moss, who was later Headmaster of Shrewsbury for many years. In his company Sandys travelled through the Black Forest to Heidelberg, and then returned to England *via* the Rhine valley and Brussels. At Schaff-

hausen Sandys wanted to consult the Codex Scaphusianus, but the librarian denied its existence, and it was
only produced after the following conversation, held in
Latin, as Sandys was at this time still learning to talk
German. In the diary Sandys writes:

I talked to the Under-librarian, making enquiries for the
Codex Scaphusianus of Isocrates. "Habesne codicem Scaphu-
sianum Isocratis?" "Isocratis—oratoris Attici? Nullus, credo,
hic existit codex Scaphusianus." "En ipsum nomen in hoc
libro scriptum." (Under-librarian goes to search the cupboards:
shews us a small room where a number of the more valuable
books are kept.) "Nonne catalogum habes codicum in hac
bibliotheca conservatorum?" "Scriptus catalogus existebat,
sed, ubi sit, nescio." "Cantabrigiae haud ita pridem omnium
fere manuscriptorum catalogum confecimus et typis excuden-
dum curavimus."

So enjoyable did this tour prove and so helpful to his
research, that Sandys made plans for a return to the
Continent next year; but this wish was not fulfilled till
1875. For the ability shown by Sandys in his work in
the College had already won him the confidence of his
colleagues and of the Master, Dr Bateson. And in
March 1870 Sandys was offered the post of College
Tutor:

My dear Sir, *March 16. 1870. St John's Lodge Cambridge.*

At the meeting of Master and Seniors this morning it was
agreed to invite you to accept the office of College Tutor, which
Dr Wood will vacate at Michaelmas next.

It will be particularly agreeable to me, if you can accept this
invitation.
Believe me
yours very truly
W. H. BATESON.

Thus at the unusually early age of twenty-five Sandys shouldered the onerous duties of College Tutor, and he carried them out conscientiously during the next thirty years. For a man of less vivid mental energy than Sandys, the acceptance of this office would have placed severe limits on the extent of his research work; but it is a remarkable proof of his fecundity that Sandys was able to combine his College work and his duties as Public Orator with a considerable output of scholastic research. As College Tutor, he soon became engaged in University business. Dr Bateson was at this time a leading figure in University administration: he headed the movement for reform, which had introduced the Statutes of 1860. Sandys, although by nature cautious, gave whole-hearted support to such innovations as he considered were demanded by the changing conditions of his time. This deep-seated conservatism tempered by the broad-mindedness, which made him recognise the need for change, when the time for it was ripe, lent special importance to his opinions.

When J. S. Reid wrote of Sandys as College Tutor, he commended the words used by the writer of the memoir, which appeared in *The Times* as an obituary notice. "To the ordinary man he was cold, impassive, ineffective and unintelligible, not quite human. As a matter of fact he was by nature intensely generous, affectionate and warm-hearted." Mr Reid went on to endorse that opinion, stating that it was fully substantiated by the reminiscences of Sandys' generosity and interest, which members of St John's College had afforded him. The same writer in *The Times* finds the reason for Sandys' coldness in his restraint.

23

He never let himself go; as a result, though he was always strictly conscientious and just, he was not effective. His lectures (one of his pupils records) were monuments of learning, and delivered with a faultlessness of diction, like his talk, which made one long for a piece of bad grammar or an anacoluthon. In private tuition he did not tell one much; instead, he always told one where the information was to be got. He had, naturally enough, favourites among his pupils. "Do you know so-and-so?" he once asked, naming one of them—"Then I congratulate you." He never forgot them, and though he kept no memoranda he could run through the career of any of them if provoked.

It was not that Sandys lacked the power of insight into human character: he was an excellent judge of men. Nor did he fail to understand and sympathise with those of his pupils who fell into financial or other trouble: among the correspondence, which has been collected for this memoir, there is a letter to Sandys thanking him for advancing a considerable sum of money to one who had been in financial difficulties, while resident at St John's College; a letter in which the sentence occurs "now that I have left Cambridge, I feel that I am better able to judge your great kindness than when I was an undergraduate". This sentiment is no doubt a commonplace among those to whom time has brought greater understanding, but in the case of Sandys' pupils it is perhaps revealing. For his weakness as a Tutor lay not in his heart but in his manner; and the undergraduate is often hasty in drawing his conclusions from externals. There was undoubtedly about Sandys a certain stiffness and staidness which pervaded not only his oratory but also his ordinary diction. On one occasion, when he was unable to open a suitcase containing literature for the illustration of his lecture, he apologised to his class, so one of the pupils records, in the words: "Gentlemen, I crave your indulgence: I go seek the aid of a locksmith". This rigidity of manner was commonly misconstrued into priggishness or conceit—a misconstruction as natural as it was erroneous. In reality it arose from the sense not of his own importance but of the importance of his office. He had the serious, almost pompous, outlook on life and its duties which characterised the earlier Victorian era: his father was deeply imbued with it, and Dr Pears and Mr Latham had noticed and encouraged the same spirit in the son. As Sandys aged, he changed very little, but, as years passed, his manner appeared less and less natural to the eyes of younger generations. This manner certainly handicapped the effectiveness of Sandys as a Tutor: to it he owed in part the gravitas and dignitas, which raised his performance of the duties of Public Orator to so high a level of attainment. And the same sense of honourableness, which was reflected in his outward manner, imparted to his scholastic work that unique flavour, so reminiscent of Renaissance scholarship. But those who knew him intimately found in him a great warmth of affection; one of his former pupils wrote of Sandys' personality in the following words:

Of his personal qualities it is difficult to speak. Not many people guessed how much genuine affection and real kindliness his rather shy disposition led to his protecting under cover of a rather formal manner. But among his pupils and friends there are those who look back to a long series of kindnesses, to gifts of valuable and useful books, to the little thoughts that show realisation of the other man's needs and difficulties, to sudden little sentences that revealed in a quick and fugitive gleam something of the older man's heart—sentences that stayed with the younger man as a picture of the real Orator.

During the five years following the election of Sandys to a Tutorship there is little to record. He was for those years on the board of examiners for the Classical Tripos, and his judgment was always steady and trustworthy according to the opinion expressed by one of his fellow examiners. In some of his vacations he took pupils in Cambridge, and in 1872 he brought out his second edition of Isocrates, *Ad Demonicum et Panegyricus*. He found himself therefore unable to obtain sufficient time to resume his travels on the Continent, and when he was away from Cambridge he either stayed with his relations or visited the English Lakes and the Dales of Yorkshire. He also stayed with his Repton friends, the Bagshawes, in Derbyshire, and later with Will Bagshawe at Uppingham, when he became a master at Uppingham School. He formed and cemented at this time a life-long friendship with H. W. Simpkinson, who came into residence at St John's College in October 1872; they spent the Easter vacation of 1875 together in the Isle of Wight, visiting Sandown and Ventnor, and in September 1875 he visited the home of Mr Simpkinson at North Creake, Norfolk. Other friends with whom he travelled at this time were Mr H. W. Moss, his companion in Germany, and Mr Freeman of St John's College, with whom he spent the July of 1875 in Scotland.

In 1871 the Rev. Timothy Sandys, the father of John Edwin, brought his family home to England, having passed the previous forty-one years in India except for an occasional furlough. Now that Sandys was in an independent position he gave all the financial assistance that he could to his father and his sister. Two of the elder brothers of John Edwin had already died at an early age, the eldest, Timothy, of fever at Howrah in 1864, where he was a Government clerk, and the second son at Delhi on the first day of the Indian Mutiny under circumstances which we have already recounted. The only surviving brother by the first marriage of Mr Sandys was Joseph Samuel, some six years the senior of John Edwin; after taking his B.A. at Corpus Christi College, Cambridge, Samuel had taken Holy Orders and served as an Army Chaplain in India. John Edwin also had four sisters, of whom the three youngest had died in childhood. The fourth, Priscilla, had married in 1862 the Rev. R. Reynolds Winter, of the S.P.G. Mission, Delhi, to whom she bore three sons and three daughters. Of the second marriage of Mr Sandys were born two sons and two daughters, James Stuart, who graduated at St John's College, Cambridge, and was later Vice-Consul at Lamu, Zanzibar, and Edward Theodore, who also graduated at St John's College, Cambridge, and became a C.M.S. Missionary at Calcutta; the two daughters by this second marriage were Isabella Mary and Emily Guthrie, neither of whom married. As the children of the second marriage were too old to remain with safety in India, Mr Sandys decided to bring them home in 1871. The following letter from Mr Sandys to his son mentions these plans and thanks him for his help to the family.

My dear Edwin,

Some time ago Samuel paid me at your desire the sum of two hundred and fifty rupees, and I am afraid I have not yet acknowledged the receipt of it, which I certainly ought to have done long ere now, with my best thanks. I doubt not that Priscilla with her young family and the necessity of her going for a while to the Hills at Simla for the benefit of her health, found what you sent her very acceptable and useful. She has lately returned to Delhi, and I trust is benefited by the change she has had at Simla.

Samuel has hitherto enjoyed good health at Dum-Dum. It is very convenient and pleasant his being stationed there, as we often have the opportunity of seeing each other. He comes here usually every second Sunday evening and returns on Tuesday morning, and I go to the Bengali Prayer Book Revising Committee in Calcutta almost every Wednesday, where I occasionally see him and sometimes I visit some native schools which lie beyond Dum-Dum, and then I have the opportunity of calling to see him in his own abode. He is thinking of paying a visit to Mussouree for about two months to officiate in the hills, where it is considered very healthy and bracing, and which place is served by chaplains going there for a couple of months each.

You will be glad to learn that we are all in good health with the exception of dear Mama who is not at all strong although she is able to get through much business and correspondence involved in her duty as Secretary and Treasurer of the Normal and Central Female Schools. It seems likely that we shall leave for England sometime next March or thereabouts. We have not yet quite fixed on the time. Emmie is now ten years old, and it is quite time that she was at home in a colder climate, and Eddie is six years old—and will be all the better for being among English children and in a colder climate, and I trust that with the Divine blessing we shall be the better for the change.

Trusting you continue well and have the Divine blessing resting on you in the discharge of your duties,

with our united love,

I am ever

your very affectionate father

T. SANDYS.

Mr Sandys returned to England in March 1871, but on November 8 he died as the result of injuries sustained in a carriage accident in Lincolnshire. He lived only a few days after the accident. He left behind him a remarkable record of service to the missionary cause, which was to be a living inspiration to John Edwin and his brothers and sisters. His loss was deeply felt in Calcutta; the following extract from the papers relating to his death is the noblest testimonial of a life devoted to the service of his fellow men.

Calcutta Corr. Committee. December 8th 1871.

On this their first meeting since the tidings of the lamented decease of their Senior Missionary, which took place at Billinghay Lincolnshire on the eighth of last month, the Committee record their admiration for the simplicity of his character and work as a missionary, and their gratitude for the long career of usefulness vouchsafed to him in India. Since his first arrival in Bengal in June 1830 until his departure on an intended furlough to England in March last Mr Sandys was permitted to labour perseveringly and with unflagging and cheerful industry in the work to which he had devoted his life. His solid worth, evenness of temper, and unselfish disposition won for him the respect and affection of all classes. His name had become a household word in Bengal both among the native Christians, who regarded him as the father of the Mission, and among many others, who had come under his influence as their instructor and knew him as their kind and considerate friend and benefactor. His cherished hope was to return to and end his days in India, but his Master had better things in store for him, and by a fatal accident, while on his way to plead the cause of the Society in a distant part of the country, he was suddenly removed from the scene of earthly toil and suffering to enter into the joy of his Lord.

Names more conspicuous may adorn the annals of the Society, but assuredly none ever more consistently illustrated the most essential features of the missionary character, undecaying faith in the promises of God and a "patient continuance in well-doing". They deeply sympathise with his bereaved widow and orphaned children thus suddenly deprived of their earthly stay and pray that the consolations of Christ may abound toward them.

With the death of Mr Sandys, the responsibility of fathering and educating his young half-brothers and half-sisters fell upon the shoulders of John Edwin. He showed himself most generous both with his money and his time, and earned the deep affection of the children by his unfailing kindness. His step-mother, who was broken-hearted on the loss of her husband, often refers to John Edwin in her letters as her "abiding support and comfort" during the ensuing years. In several of the vacations from 1872 to 1875 he stayed with the family or took them away for holidays; and in 1875 he accompanied his half-sister Emily to Germany, where she was sent to school.

Sandys' close association with Repton was also maintained; his affection for Dr Pears and Mr Latham caused him to visit the school on several occasions. He also reported on Repton for the School Enquiry Commission; in that report he traces briefly the history of the school, and it is interesting to notice that Repton stood fifth in the number of endowed schools with regard to the number of students and also of scholars resident at Oxford and Cambridge. The success of the school, as Sandys points out in his report, was largely due to the headmaster, Dr Pears, during the first five years of whose régime, from 1854 to 1859, the number of boys rose from forty-seven to one hundred and twenty-seven, and later to over two hundred. In 1873 Dr Pears retired from Repton and two years later he died; Sandys played a prominent part in the raising of subscriptions for the establishment of a memorial suitable to the commemoration of his unexampled services to the school, and he himself, at the request of Dr Pears' successor, Dr Huckin, composed the Latin inscription dedicated to his memory. Sandys was also President for many years of the Old Reptonian Society in Cambridge and took a personal interest in such Reptonians as came to St John's College.

In the summer of 1872 Sandys examined Shrewsbury School, from which there was an annual Exhibition to St John's College, and thus began an association with that school, which lasted throughout his lifetime. The headmaster was then Mr Moss, an intimate friend of Sandys, and the Bishop of Lichfield, the senior Governor of the school, was a Fellow of St John's. In thanking Sandys for his "very clear, full, and satisfactory report on Shrewsbury", the Bishop refers to the "revival of learning", which had placed Shrewsbury in the forefront of English schools, and which was maintained under the headmastership of Mr Moss.

Despite the stress of business in which Sandys had been involved in the last few years, he had not been idle in the matter of research. After re-editing his Isocrates in 1872, he turned his attention to the *Private Orations* of Demosthenes and decided to publish twelve of them with the collaboration of that distinguished scholar F. A. Paley. The speeches were published in two volumes, Sandys being mainly responsible for the second, and the work was primarily intended for use of students at schools and at the universities. When the resolution was first made, Mr Paley wrote the following letter to Sandys which shows the extent of their collaboration.

My dear Sandys,   *July* 9 1872. 17 *Botolph Lane.*

   I should like to hear your ideas on our proposed *Private Orations*, and also which of them you design to take. The question is, of course, entirely open as to the number and the selection. I left at your rooms yesterday a paper with a list of twelve, that I myself know best. If you will definitely commit to my care any portion I will get it in hand as soon as I have any time. Just now I am rather busy in re-editing Propertius, which however is more than half printed.
   I suggest our notes should be rather numerous than long. A few explanatory words, with neat and accurate renderings, will be more acceptable in general, than longer and more learned notes. But I shall gladly take your advice in the matter.
   I am so engaged with pupils (thanks to you in part), that I can hardly propose just now a time for a "conference", but I hope we shall get a walk before long.

                            Believe me
                               very sincerely yours

                            F. A. PALEY.

The first volume which was mainly the work of Mr Paley, was published in 1874, and it was followed in 1875 by the second volume. By these works Sandys confirmed and enhanced the reputation for sound scholarship, already won by his edition of Isocrates; and while the latter had aroused interest only amongst English scholars, the *Private Orations* by the fact of their filling an obvious gap in the ranks of classical literature were received not with a provincial but with a wide and universal acclamation. Of the *Private Orations* there was only one edition in English, by Mr Penrose, and that had long since been out of print; in Germany several general editions of Demosthenes, including the important works of Arnold, Schaefer, and Blass, had been produced in recent years, but no separate edition had been published of these difficult speeches. Of their reception in England it suffices to quote *The Saturday Review*: "It is long since we have come upon a work evincing more pains, scholarship, and varied research and illustration than Mr Sandys' contribution to the Private Orations of Demosthenes". In the preparation of this work Sandys had undertaken the study and collation of German publications on the subject, and this brought him into contact with some eminent German scholars; of these Professor F. Blass became a close friend of Sandys after staying with him in Cambridge in 1874. Blass was at this time engaged in editing the important third volume of his *Attische Beredsamkeit*, which treated of Demosthenes, and in 1888–9 he re-edited the Dindorf text of Demosthenes. On returning to Germany after his visit to Cambridge he writes thanking Sandys for his hospitality.

Those three days I spent with you were, beyond all doubt, the happiest I had this time in England, and really very happy days, when I had everything I could wish excepting my wife to share the pleasure. And with reference to the next volume of *Attische Beredsamkeit*, one thing more; don't give yourself trouble about ordering my new book: because its brothers have had with you so splendid a reception, and enjoy so much honour, it will come to you voluntarily, as soon as it can. It regards that as a duty owed to you, I dare say.

This is typical of the friendships which Sandys' courtesy and hospitality won him among Continental scholars; when travelling abroad he made a point of calling on any with whom his work had brought him into contact; he gained thereby that width of mind and international understanding which saved him from the animosities of the Great War and made him one of the leading figures in the Society for the Entente of Literature. With many of his friends he corresponded in Latin letters of true Ciceronian polish. An example is afforded by his correspondence with Dr Otto Schneider:

Viro doctissimo Othoni Schneider
Johannes Edvinus Sandys
S.

Demosthenicarum orationum a me nuperrime editarum exemplar, sicut eo die promisi, quo iucunde apud te eram, hodie ad te mittendum iussi; quod quidem non modo testem communium studiorum sed hospitii etiam et in te tuosque amicitiae pignus quantulumcunque futurum esse spero. Simul editoris misi imaginem, severius fortasse quam verius expressam; nec non uxori tuae optimae chartulas aliquot, quae collegiorum nostrorum speciem externam paullo fidelius referant. Ceterum nunc maxime ad sororem meam, quam uti meministi non procul a te mense Septembri reliqui, volumus circa Saturnaliorum tempus, sicut non in Anglia tantum sed plus etiam in Germania assolet, strenas aliquot mittendas curare, quae ne ob itineris longioris incommodum vix satis tuto (ne dicam maiore sumptu quam, ut in re tam levi, opus est) istuc perveniant, pergratum matri eius et mihi ipsi erit, si uxor tua pro sua benignitate, e pecunia cum his litteris missa, in usum sororis meae et amicae eius quam eodem tempore inter Moravienses reliqui, ipsa conquirere velit et circa diem xx Dec. nostro nomine munuscula aliquot mittere, sicut bellaria cupedia, et unum et alterum libellum, vel picturas, vel nugas alias non prorsus inutiles; denique meo nomine elegantioris formae (ut verbo Graeco utar) θερμόμετρον quod sorori meae a penatibus longe remotae fraterni foci, fraterni etiam qui numquam friget amoris memoriam conservet, et inter hiemis Germanicae frigora quotidie suadeat θερμὴν ἐπὶ ψυχροῖσι καρδίαν τρέφειν.

Uxori tuae salutem quam plurimam.

Dabam Cantabrigiae
apud Coll. Div. Johannis
Id. Nov. MDCCCLXXV.

To this request with regard to Sandys' half-sister Emily Dr Schneider acceded in the following letter:

Doctissimo viro
Johanni Edvino Sandys
Otto Schneider
S.

His ipsis diebus allatae mihi sunt litterae tuae comitatis et liberalitatis plenae, quibus quod addere voluisti non solum imaginem tuam, sed etiam a te editas Demosthenis aliquot orationes, eruditissimum hercle opus, quanto me putas affectum gaudio? Et librum quidem tuum quoties in usum meum quantum potero convertam simulque imaginem tuam illam intuebor os vultumque tuum fidelissime, si quid video, repraesentantem, toties libenter in memoriam iucundi eius diei redeam, quo praesentem te videre et tecum confabulari mihi licuit. Quibus beneficiis persuasum habe me obstrictum esse et semper me ubicunque volueris gratissimum tibi fore. Sed non minus laetatus sum quod (quae mea erat apud te fiducia) sorori tuae

3-2

strenas aliquot aptas emi tradique nomine tuo a me volebas
addita qua emerem pecunia. Peragam autem quae iussisti
quanta potero cum fide adhibita opera uxoris meae, quae et
ipsa ob transmissas a te sibi imagunculas Cantabrigienses gratias
agere gestiebat. At de hoc negotio mox iterum ad te scribam
ubi pecuniae rationem reddam: interim vale meque uti facis
amare perge.

      Dabam Gothae a.d. x Cal. Decembr. MDCCCLXXV.

The courteous and sincere cordiality, which converted
the nodding acquaintances met in the field of classical
research into warm and enduring friendships, accounts
in part for the international reputation of Sandys as a
scholar: for while this reputation was primarily due to
the distinction of his scholastic work, he had avoided the
acrimonious dogmatism engendered by a narrow provincial outlook, which can sour the streams of thought
and impede the advancement of knowledge by introducing a polemic spirit into a subject essentially humane.

In the autumn of 1875 Sandys had held his Fellowship for eight years and was now thirty-one years of age;
he had already fulfilled, and even surpassed, the hopes
entertained for him by his friends at the time of his
election. His editions of Isocrates and Demosthenes
had placed him in the forefront of a new generation of
Cambridge scholarship and had won him an early recognition among both English and Continental scholars.
His success was the more notable because he had not
sacrificed his duties in the College and in the University
to the furtherance of his own reputation as a scholar.
Of his services to the College as Tutor we have already
written: suffice it to say that during these and following
years he entered fully into the life of the College and

formed friendships with many of his pupils which lasted throughout his life. He was also a lecturer at both St John's and Jesus Colleges, and in 1876 he completed a period of five years in the office of Examiner for the Classical Tripos; in both of these capacities he had shown an outstanding ability which won from one of his colleagues the ejaculation "really, my dear Sandys, none but yourself could be your parallel!"

Of the influence of these eight years on his personality there is little evidence to be found in the few private letters which have been preserved from this time. He had been shy as a boy and he remained so throughout his life. Moreover it would seem that the responsibilities which he had shouldered at so early an age had developed in Sandys more quickly than in most men a purposefulness and dignity, which tended to conceal from his pupils the warmth of his affection and the width of his sympathies and to invest his relations with his contemporaries with a certain formality and reserve. But this element in his character was destined to fit him for an office, the long tenure of which conferred upon him many distinctions.

CHAPTER III

1876   1880

IN 1876 Sir Richard Jebb, a personal friend of
Sandys, resigned the office of Public Orator, which
he had held since 1869, to become Professor of
Greek at Glasgow University. The two candidates for
the office were Sandys and Mr Charles Walter Moule
of Corpus Christi College, who was bracketed Senior
Classic in 1857 and was known to his contemporaries as
one of the finest exponents of the art of writing Latin
Verse who ever appeared in Cambridge. Sandys' qualifications were strengthened by the special attention he
had devoted to the subject of Greek and Roman oratory
in his published works and in his College lectures:
moreover his personal bearing and dignified manner
were eminently suited to the post. Sandys was supported by a very strong committee, which included
several Heads of Houses and Headmasters of schools,
with Dr Bateson, the Master of St John's College, as
Chairman.

The election took place on October 17, 1876, and particular arrangements were made for the unprecedented
number of voters who attended. The railway companies
ran special late trains to London, stopping at inter-
mediate stations, and most of the colleges provided
entertainment for the "out-voters". No fewer than
1288 members of the Senate recorded their votes—the
largest poll on record for a one-day election. Sandys
was elected by a small majority to be Public Orator in

the University of Cambridge, a post which he held for forty-three years, thus constituting another record in length of service.

As Public Orator, Sandys carried out his duties with scrupulous care, and took special care always to make himself thoroughly conversant with the careers of those whom he presented for honorary degrees. While his knowledge was in itself a compliment to the presentees, the excellence of the miniature character-paintings which he wrought lend a special interest to the collection of speeches and epistles which he edited in May 1910 under the title of *Orationes et Epistolae Cantabrigienses* (1876–1909). And it was especially this feature in his speeches which won for him so many letters of thanks from those whom he commemorated: to quote only from one letter, that of Matthew Arnold, written in 1883: "A thousand thanks for the printed copies of your speeches which you have so kindly sent me. I am glad the speeches are in this permanent form. For myself, I can only say that I wish the next age (if the next age inquires at all about me) to read no other and no longer character of me than yours". The acquiring of the information he desired often entailed much labour and research, but until the last few years of his office, when the conclusion of the Great War flooded him with work, he never complained of his burden. For he was always interested in those whom he met, whether as recipients of honorary degrees or as acquaintances in humbler walks of life: and he brought to his own love of research an acute power of observation and a splendid memory.

Of the occasions on which he made speeches and of the graceful Latinity of the speeches themselves we shall speak later. In the matter of style he followed that of his predecessor and friend, Sir Richard Jebb, affecting an ornate and highly polished diction as opposed to that of W. G. Clark which had been very terse and restrained. Of the speeches the writer of an obituary notice of Sandys in *The Times* says that they were perhaps open to the criticism that they were sometimes unduly dry, but that their diction and their taste were impeccable. This dryness or lack of humour arose mainly from the respect with which he regarded the position of Public Orator: he felt that these occasions were marked by a special solemnity and he never let himself go further than an occasional pun. In general also his wit was restrained rather than hilarious, but the neatness with which he expressed himself often added a spice to his jokes. On one occasion when he was told that a certain famous headmaster, who was an enthusiastic lepidopterist, had rushed into his Sixth Form room waving a butterfly-net and crying out "capui, capui", Sandys replied: "I always said that so-and-so was no mere scholar".

Sandys, as we should expect, was ever conscious of the weight of tradition behind his office, and his earnestness was in part due to the desire to show himself worthy of that heritage. "It is natural", wrote J. S. Reid, "and in accordance with the predilections of Sandys throughout his life that a great part of his satisfaction in his success was due to the reflection that, as Public Orator, he was continuing a line of famous scholars, among whom were Erasmus, Sir John Cheke and Roger

Ascham (these two being members of St John's College), also George Herbert, W. G. Clark, and Sir Richard Jebb." It was not an unfitting reward that one who honoured so highly and maintained so steadfastly the traditions of the Public Orator, should on his retirement be awarded the title of Orator Emeritus and be known always to those of his own generation as "the Orator".

As Public Orator, Sandys was also *ex officio* an adjudicator of the Porson and of several other University Prizes, and an examiner for the University Scholarships. Despite these additions to his former routine of work, Sandys was able to revise and edit a Commentary on the *Rhetoric* of Aristotle, which had been left in a nearly completed form by Mr Cope and entrusted to him by the executors on the advice of two distinguished Fellows of Trinity College; the Commentary was published in three volumes by the University Press in 1877.

In the summer of that year he went with his half-sisters and his eldest brother, an Army Chaplain in India, on a two months' tour to the Continent. In his diary he mentions that the occasion, on which they met at Neudietendorf, was the first time that they had been together. Thence they went to Munich *via* Saxon Switzerland and then to Pontresina, returning to Antwerp by Zurich, Geneva, Heidelberg and the Moselle. His diary of this tour is a remarkable illustration of the width of his interests; while studying classical manuscripts wherever he came across them and tracing the course of Roman roads, on the Albula Pass for instance, he was equally interested in mediaeval battlefields, weapons and monuments, in painting, sculpture and church architecture—and these not with the superficiality of the average sightseer; for with Sandys interest meant that curiosity went hand-in-hand with knowledge. Much of their time also was spent in walking in the Black Forest and in the Swiss Alps. In the following summer Sandys visited the Italian Lakes and Venice, returning by the Via Mala to England; in the course of this tour he studied the collection of manuscripts at the Doge's Palace, and was especially interested in the tenth and eleventh century manuscripts of Demosthenes' speeches.

In 1879 Sandys was offered an important post in Canada by one who thought that a man of Sandys' youth and ability would exert an important influence on the educational progress of a colony which was then rapidly growing. Sandys, however, refused the offer, feeling doubtless that he owed more to his own University after his appointment as Public Orator. Cambridge afforded greater opportunities for the pursuit of the research which was his main interest; and he was probably also unwilling to resign so soon the important position won him by his distinction in England. Moreover his influence on education in England was already considerable, and one of his most important works from the educational point of view was on the eve of publication.

This work was "The *Bacchae* of Euripides with critical and explanatory notes and with numerous illustrations from works of ancient art", published in 1880. The importance of this edition lay largely in the attention paid to the influences which affected the play. Hitherto the value of adding the artistic background to the text of an ancient work had not been sufficiently realised; for this reason Sandys' edition at once became popular in schools and in universities. This aspect of the edition was stressed by the reviewers; for instance in *The Academy* we read:

Mr Sandys has set an example which it is to be hoped will be followed by other editors of Greek tragic poets. That is to say, besides the purely literary part of such a task, he has apparently spared no pains in collecting from ancient works of art illustrations of passages in the play. It is evident also that he has done this not as a mere matter of curiosity, in the manner of the old dilettanti, but on a principle which recognises Euripides as having been on the one hand influenced by the arts of his time, and on the other himself a source of influence and impetus to artists after his day. In most cases the engravings are good, while the information concerning them is complete, but is conveyed in a way to give pleasure to those who are interested in ancient art as well as in literature.

Dr N. Wecklein in the *Philologischer Anzeiger* of 1881 wrote:

Diese des schönen Stücks würdige Ausgabe kann man nur mit grossem Wohlgefallen betrachten. Der Eindruck der herrlichen Ausstattung wird erhöht durch die über das ganze Buch an passenden Stellen vertheilten trefflichen Illustrationen. Der Verfasser hat überhaupt die archäologischen Beziehungen des Stücks in der Einleitung eine ausführliche Besprechung gewidmet, worin wir nicht den geringsten Vorzug der Ausgabe sehen.

The *Bacchae* passed quickly into a second edition.

On August 17, 1880, Sandys married Mary Grainger Hall, whose father, the Rev. Henry Hall, M.A., had since 1863 been Vicar of St Paul's, Cambridge. Mr Hall graduated at Magdalene College, Cambridge, and was elected to a Fellowship there for four years; he was for three years private chaplain to Lord Monson, during which time he resided in Italy or Switzerland, and from 1845–62 was Headmaster of St Albans Grammar School. During his ministry in Cambridge he won the respect and affection of his parishioners and was especially influential in the affairs of Addenbrooke's Hospital, of which he became a Select Governor in 1871. As a token of the respect in which his memory was held by his parishioners, the Union Jack during Jubilee week, the time of his death and his funeral, was lowered to half-mast on the tower of St Paul's Church. After the wedding Mr and Mrs Sandys went for a tour in Germany, Switzerland and France, the first of the many tours which they made together until the last years of Sir John's life. In Miss Hall Sandys found tastes and interests which were very congenial with his own, for she shared his appreciation of classical art and literature; and, after the death of Sir John, Lady Sandys made a gift, in accordance with his wish, of 1800 volumes from her husband's library to the Archaeological Museum. They resided in Cambridge at 145 Chesterton Road for three years, and then at Merton House in Queen's Road until 1913, when they moved to St John's House, which was built for Sir John in Grange Road. For many years Sir John and Lady Sandys were distinguished members of Cambridge society, and on several occasions attended the levées and drawing rooms at the Courts of Queen Victoria and of King Edward.

CHAPTER IV

1880   1900

D URING these years it is not possible nor would
it be profitable to trace chronologically the events
of Sandys' life. For he had now encountered
the main influences which moulded his character and
his subsequent career; his work in Cambridge as Public
Orator and as Tutor and Lecturer at St John's College
(he had resigned his position of Lecturer at Jesus College
on his assumption of the Public Oratorship) left him but
little time for the pursuit of his own studies, and his
vacations were dedicated either to the preparation of his
works for publication or to travels abroad in the company of Mrs Sandys. Of all these activities he has left
traces which enrich his memory and bear testimony to
the remarkable productivity of these busy years—a productivity which aroused the surprise of his colleagues,
expressed for instance in the following letter:

Jan. 26 1894. Magdalene College, Cambridge
My dear Sandys,

I am sorry I can be of no use to you for your College examinations. We have our own at the end of this term and I am
immersed in the Tripos in June, and I know I shall find them
enough for a somewhat *debile corpus*.

Will you some day impart to me "in strict confidence" the
secret of how you manage to combine social παιδιά, enormous
literary σπουδή and no end of official, tutorial, or oratorical
activity?

Yours very truly,

W. A. GILL

45

In Sandys' edition of *Orationes et Epistolae Cantabrigienses*, which is itself a selection of speeches actually made, we find for these twenty years no less than three hundred orations. The following were among the most distinguished of those whom he presented during this time: their Royal Highnesses the late Duke of Clarence, and the late Duke of Edinburgh, and his Majesty the late King of Sweden; also Lord Acton, Lord Rosebery, Joseph Chamberlain, Matthew Arnold, Lord Randolph Churchill, Sir Andrew Clark, Sir Alexander Grant, Professor Helmholtz, Professor Jowett, Professor Maitland, Lord Rosse, Lord Russell of Killowen, Lord Salisbury, Archbishop Temple, Sir Richard Temple, Mr G. F. Watts, Professor Adams, Sir John Evans, Sir George Stokes, Asa Gray, Simon Newcomb, Kowalevsky, Mendeléef, Oliver Wendell Holmes, Sir Henry Irving, Professor Norton, Sir John Seeley, Dvořák, Grieg, and Tschaikowsky. Nor was the delivery of these speeches by any means easy, as the following extract from *The Daily Graphic* of May 15, 1900, shows:

King Oscar of Sweden and Norway became yesterday a Doctor of Cambridge University and learnt by practical experience what the historic ceremony of conferring honorary degrees in the Cambridge Senate House is like. As his was the only degree to be conferred, and as the present time is mid-term rather than that joyous period in June when all examinations are finished and all results known, it might have been feared that the number of undergraduates who grace the galleries on such occasions would have been severely diminished. That was not the case, however. The Senate House, resplendent with a new roof, was filled with what we may describe as quite a June chorus; and if the flashes of undergraduate wit were less perceptible than the flow of undergraduate spirits, the welcomes which King Oscar received were warm enough to compensate for any such deficiency....The progress to the dais was in a double sense a Royal one, for the King, clearly gratified by the warmth of the greeting which met him, bowed again and again to the gallery, and each bow fired a fresh train of cheers. The cheers began again when the King rose to take his place opposite the Chancellor at the foot of the dais and to listen to the recital of his qualifications in the rotund Latin of the Public Orator. The Public Orator's sentences were received in the usual manner. "Scandinaviae regem insignem hodie libenter salutamus", began Dr Sandys, and a voice from the gallery cried "Steady!" "Militum Napoleoneorum ("I beg your pardon", said someone in the gallery, politely; "But would you mind repeating that?") —Napoleoneorum ducis generosissimi nepotem," went on the Public Orator, firmly, and pressed on despite loud complaints as to his quantities. The King was evidently a little puzzled at first by the ebullitions of the gallery, but at last he entered into the spirit of the thing and smiled too—then the gallery cheered him indeed. Never has the flattering phrase been more continuously cheered. When the Public Orator came to the sentence which described the candidate as "artis musicae et Musarum cultorem eximium, oratorem egregium, rerum denique militarium et navalium scriptorem eruditissimum", King Oscar, still in the spirit of the thing, shook his head in smiling deprecation of the compliment, but the undergraduates endorsed the observations of Dr Sandys with three cheers and the remark that he had not said half enough. A reference to the war, coupled with the name of the Colonies, gave a fresh starting point for enthusiasm, and the oration ended in a blaze of triumph by a reference to the King as the friend of Britain and the British Empire.

But on most occasions the dignity of his bearing and the resonance of his voice commanded the attention even of an undergraduate audience, which was in those

47

days appreciative of neat Latinity. In *The Daily Graphic* of June 14, 1893, we read:

The Maharajah of Bhaonagar was the first to be called forth. Dr Sandys, standing beside his victim, who was clad in rich red and gold robes of his own, as well as in the doctor's gown and hood, began his oration ore rotundo, in such wise that every word of his Latin, pronounced in the rather heart-breaking "correct" fashion of which Dr Sandys is so distinguished an exponent, was distinctly audible and intelligible, though what the Indian prince thought it all meant does not sufficiently appear. The Public Orator has a knack of saying very neat things in very sounding phrases, and he seems to enjoy them in the spirit of a true artist. He had the undergraduate ear yesterday. The necessary rather silly jokes from the gallery never put him out, and his points were taken almost as quickly as the points in a modern farcical comedy....When Lord Roberts rose, the house rose too, and there was a prolonged roar of cheers, which for some time checked the proceedings. Dr Sandys was frequently interrupted by bursts of applause, particularly when he alluded to the campaign in Afghanistan, and spoke of the General as "Vir qui properando restituit rem".

It is interesting to note the opening words with which Sandys in 1881 presented the Rev. Charles Taylor, who had recently been elected Master of St John's College.

Quanto dolore nuper audivit Senatus noster, conticuisse subito vocem illam, quae, vestra qui aetate et experientia antecellitis memoria, per annos novem in hoc ipso loco eloquentiae Latinae exempla egregia identidem ediderat. Quanto desiderio eundem omnes nuper prosecuti sumus, qui, postea, quattuor et viginti annos Collegium omnium consensu magnum animo neque trepido neque temerario gubernavit.

In this elegant tribute to the memory of Dr Bateson, Master of St John's College, 1857–81, and Public Orator, 1848–57, Sandys gave expression to his own personal devotion to one who, from the beginning of Sandys' days as an undergraduate, had taken a great interest in his career. In the last few words of the passage referring to Dr Bateson, his loss is beautifully expressed: "Quo sole nostro subito extincto, statim omnes intelleximus, quantum lumen occidisset".

As Public Orator, Sandys represented the University on many important occasions, as for instance on the occasion of the first Jubilee of Queen Victoria, when a University deputation visited Windsor Castle. In 1886 Sandys became a Litt.D. of Cambridge University, and on the occasion of the tercentenary of Dublin University in 1892 he received an Honorary Litt.D. at that University. He was also at this time elected a member of the Athenaeum Club by the Committee.

This was again a period of great literary activity for Sandys. After his edition of the *Bacchae* he returned to the study of Greek and Roman oratory. The first and perhaps the most important work of this period was his edition of Cicero's *Orator* in 1885. It was the first occasion on which this work of Cicero was edited with an English commentary. The edition was remarkable not only for the fullness and excellence of the annotation, but also contained a series of short essays on all periods of classical Greek oratory and on Roman oratory under the Republic. Like the *Bacchae*, this edition was illustrated by reproductions from ancient works of art connected with the subject-matter, including a bust of Cicero preserved in the museum at Madrid, then published for the first time in England. Another important innovation in this edition, which betrays the interest already taken by Sandys in mediaeval scholarship, was the attention given to the history of the manuscripts and the early editions of the *Orator*. The frontispiece represented a page of the chief manuscript, the "codex Abrincensis", and the introduction contained the opening sentences of the first printed edition of the *Orator* (by Omnibonus Leonicenus in 1485 at Venice) with quotations from Poggio, Victor Pisanus and Strebaeus. In the words of J. S. Reid "this work displayed all the special qualities and tastes of the editor's scholarship".

In 1890 an annotated text of the speech of Demosthenes against the Law of Leptines with a facsimile of the Paris manuscript was published, "a worthy representative", according to *The Classical Review*, "of the highest level of classical scholarship". In 1891 Sandys was joint-editor of *A Dictionary of Classical Antiquities from the German of Dr Oskar Seyffert*, his colleague being Professor Nettleship. A third edition was printed in 1894 and is still a standard work. An important aspect of the work is stressed by the reviewer in *Education*, who writes: "Its value would be hard to exaggerate for the use of sixth and fifth form boys. We unhesitatingly express our opinion that it is a most valuable work, important for both reference and comment, and one that is sure to give fresh interest to the study of the great writers in Greek and Latin Literature".

In 1893 an admirable edition of Aristotle's *Constitution of Athens* was published by Sandys. A comprehensive publication of the text with introduction, notes and illustrations was at the time required to standardise this valuable addition to surviving classical literature, and

Sandys possessed to a high degree the qualities necessary for such work—maturity and rapidity of scholarship. In the short interval between the first publication of the text by F. G. Kenyon in January 1891 and the appearance of Sandys' edition in 1893 a vast number of emendations and commentaries was published in the classical journals of all countries. This material Sandys was able to digest and summarise in the conspectus of Bibliography included in his Introduction. In settling the text Sandys consulted the *papyrus* as well as the facsimile, and contributed his own conjectures to the restoration of the text: variant readings adopted in the principal editions published before that of Sandys were recorded in the Critical Notes. The edition also contained an Introduction sketching the course of the political literature of Greece before the time of Aristotle and discussing the question of authorship, a Testimonia with a list of the quotations found in the Greek lexicographers, scholiasts and others, and Explanatory Notes comparing the new evidence with the old. Special attention was given throughout to the evidence of Greek inscriptions, and illustrations drawn from archaeological discoveries were included. The completeness and excellence of this edition set it among the most valuable of Sandys' works and make it indispensable to the modern student of the treatise.

In 1896 Sandys published a *First Greek Reader and Primer*, and revised his 1875 publication of *Select Private Orations* of Demosthenes for a third edition, the original co-editor Mr Paley having died in 1888. In 1897 and 1900 the *Philippic Orations* of Demosthenes were published by Macmillan in two parts, the first containing the First Philippic and the Olynthiacs, and the second the Speech on the Peace, the Second Philippic, the Speech on the Chersonesus, and the Third Philippic. The edition contains a historical commentary and discusses the evidence for the text, in which respect Sandys largely followed the opinions of his friend Blass. In this case too some of the speeches included had not been published in England of recent years, and Sandys did a service to classical studies in making these speeches more easily and more pleasantly available to the student.

At this time he also contributed to *The Classical Review* after its foundation in 1887, and was offered but refused the editorship of that periodical in 1898. In offering this post J. B. Mayor wrote: "I do not know anyone of wider knowledge, more accurate scholarship, and fairer judgment, and I am sure all scholars would rejoice, if you felt you could afford the time for it, either by yourself or with the assistance of a joint editor". He also contributed for several years to *Literature*, and wrote a chapter on "English Scholarship" in *Social England*, vol. VI, published in 1896.

The reputation for width and soundness of scholarship, which was acquired by Sandys through his writings, led many scholars to seek his advice and opinion. From the letters of thanks, preserved in his correspondence, it is clear that he ungrudgingly afforded any help that he was able and spared no pains in ascertaining the accuracy of his statements; his courtesy and kindness in this respect were marked features in his character, and won him many friends among both English and German scholars. Among these letters may be mentioned one from Samuel Butler, B.A., of St John's College, thanking him for his kindness in sending a number of corrigenda with reference to his book on Dr Samuel Butler, written in 1896. An important work, in which Sandys assisted, was the publication of the poems of Bacchylides by F. G. Kenyon in 1897. Mr Kenyon mentions in his Introduction the special services rendered to him by Professor Blass and Dr Sandys, and writing just before the publication of the book to Sandys he says: "I have not been able to acknowledge each instalment of your notes on Bacchylides, but now that all the proofs of the text and notes have passed through your hands, let me send you my best thanks for the help you have given me".

In addition to the duties of examining, which were incumbent on him *ex officio* as Public Orator, Sandys acted as External Examiner in Greek in the Victoria University, Manchester, for four years, and as Examiner in Greek in the University of London for the same number of years. In Cambridge he was an active member of the Philological Society, of which he was at one time President, and several of his papers are recorded in the *Proceedings* of the Society.

His connection with Repton was closely maintained. He was for many years President of the Cambridge University Old Reptonian Society, and was often the speaker at Old Reptonian dinners. Several of his friends at Repton died before the turn of the century. Dr Pears died in 1875, and Sandys' housemaster, the Rev. Edward Latham, to whom he was deeply attached, died in 1883; both the Latin inscriptions in their memory inscribed

53

on the tablets in the School chapel were composed by Sandys. The Right Hon. George Denman, who was Senior Classic in 1842 and became in 1875 a Judge of the High Court of Judicature, died in 1896; he and Sandys had been brought together by their Repton connection and had formed a close friendship. Sandys wrote an obituary notice of his friend in *The Cambridge Review* and composed the Latin inscription set up in brass to his memory in the School chapel. He also assisted his son in the publication of Greek and Latin epigrams and verses written by Mr Denman and published under the title of *Intervalla*. His visits to Repton were frequent and on more than one occasion he was asked to speak on the Repton speech-day.

Another Repton friend, whom he often visited, was the Rev. Vale Bagshawe, an assistant master at Uppingham School; Sandys used often to stay with him at Uppingham and in 1892 was present at the school production of the *Alcestis*. For Sandys was much interested in the presentation of Greek plays, and attended the performances at Bradfield College, as often as he was able. In this particular year, 1892, he saw the *Alcestis* at Uppingham, the *Agamemnon* at Bradfield, and the *Frogs* at Oxford—as interesting a trio of plays as one could find.

Of Sandys' affection for and generosity to his step-mother and her family there is abundant testimony in their letters to him. After the death of the Rev. Timothy Sandys, Mrs Sandys had come to depend largely on John Edwin for advice and help in the education of the young family; he spent many vacations with them both before and after his marriage, and in financial matters was most generous to them. In his family he suffered early bereavements. Two of his elder brothers had died before he himself was twenty years of age; in 1881 he lost his sister Priscilla to whom he was especially devoted. She died in India, where she was married to the Rev. R. R. Winter, of the Delhi Mission, and left a family of three sons and three daughters. Of his own brothers and sisters, Joseph Samuel, the third son of Mr Sandys by his first marriage, was the only one left after the death of Priscilla; he served in India as an Army Chaplain from 1868–91, when he returned to England and became Vicar of Beoley, Worcestershire, and Rector of Tickenham, Nailsea, Bristol, until his death through heart-failure in 1906; he left a widow but no issue. Of his half-brothers, John Edwin was most intimate with the eldest of the family, James Stuart, who was some six years younger than John Edwin. James Stuart Sandys took his degree at St John's College, Cambridge, and subsequently became Vice-Consul at Lamu, Zanzibar; he owed much to the affection of his brother, who had been instrumental in sending him to Harrow School and St John's College. After five years on the staff of Lancaster School, he entered the service of the British East Africa Company; he went to Africa, because he too was inspired by the missionary zeal of his father. In a letter to John Edwin in June 1889, he writes:

Dear Edwin,

At the present moment we are bowling merrily over the moonbright waters about $3\frac{1}{2}$ degrees south of the line, the good ship panting steam and heeling over under the stress of canvas.

These voyages—it is my sixth—between Zanzibar Mombasa and Lamu are very enjoyable, the sea near the equator being always fairly smooth and the weather glorious.

My seven months out here have passed away very pleasantly; the scenery both on the islands and mainland is exceedingly beautiful, the "deadly" climate to me at any rate has been very merciful, and everywhere I have met with the greatest kindness and hospitality from the English residents.

If possible I shall stay now on this side of the Continent and not go round *via* the Congo. It was the hope of eventually doing something against the Slave Trade that turned my thoughts to Africa and till a short time ago, owing to Stanley's dash and the creation of the Congo Free State, it seemed as if civilisation was going to attack the Slave system on the West just as in Gordon's time Egypt was the point d'appui—but now Fortune has skipped round to the East again. This is the sole reason of my having prolonged my stay here, and if I get any definite work to do, bringing me in contact with the Slave question, I shall stay here for some time.

We are being blockaded by no less than twenty-three men of war of various nations, but as I do not export slaves or import firearms, it does not affect me personally except that cartridges and powder are getting very dear! Off Zanzibar of course it is dangerous to go on the mainland. Only the day before yesterday a German missionary and two ladies came to my hotel, driven from Dar es Salaam and barely escaping with their lives, one of the ladies being shot in the arm; a Bavarian R.C. Mission a little further inland was attacked at the same time and everyone killed. From what is happening at Uganda and Lake Nyassa and here and the Sudan, it is evident that the Slave Dealers mean to die hard.

This was the last letter that James Stuart Sandys wrote to his brother, for in August he died of fever at Lamu. In an obituary notice in *The Lancastrian* we read:

So passed away one of the noblest hearts that ever lived; a

man who was ever unselfish, ever at the service of his friends, always a genial companion, liberal of mind, the soul of modesty and truth. Had he consented to leave his post some weeks before, when many a fever-stricken man would have desired and deserved leave of absence, his life might have been saved. But no, there was press of work, and he was not the man to leave it undone. Nothing could be more characteristic. The self-denial which so strongly marked his life was perhaps in some degree the cause of his death—a noble infirmity and a noble mind.

A tablet was erected in his memory at the School chapels of Harrow and Lancaster.

The only surviving members of the family were the three youngest children by Mr Sandys' second marriage, to whom John Edwin stood in the position of a father: Mary Isabella, Emily Guthrie and Edward Theodore. Of these the last was a M.A. of St John's College and became a C.M.S. Missionary in Calcutta; he married twice and had five children. Neither of his sisters married, and one of them undertook missionary work. In the lives of the Sandys family one can see the same influences and ideals at work as moulded the character of John Edwin. His life was set in a different scene from theirs, but his personality bore the same distinctive trait of unselfish and unsparing devotion to duty.

In the company of his wife, Sandys travelled abroad in one or more of the vacations each year throughout these twenty years. Some of these tours were dictated by the need to consult important manuscripts, as for instance a tour to Normandy to consult the "codex Abrincensis" in September 1884; but even when he was travelling for pleasure, he always made a point of visiting any library which contained early manuscripts. As we have noticed in regard to his scholastic work,

Sandys never underestimated the importance of the artistic background of a nation's history; he realised the close relation that exists between a nation's artistic and literary output, and he saw that no history of an ancient civilisation could be complete without a consideration of its cultural standards. It was in this respect that Sandys showed a wider range of vision than contemporary scholars in Cambridge: he recognised at once the importance of the discovery of Schliemann, and he saw that the study of archaeology formed an essential part of the understanding of classical culture. Therein lay the importance of his edition of the *Bacchae*, where for the first time this side of the subject was adequately treated. And during his travels he assiduously visited local museums and ancient remains; his interest embraced not only classical archaeology but also Byzantine and mediaeval archaeology, as the history and art of these periods had, ever since his days at Repton, been a matter of interest to him. His enthusiasm for painting and church architecture especially were shared by Mrs Sandys, who used to sketch and paint when she accompanied him abroad.

Down to the year 1894 Sandys was in the habit of keeping a diary of his travels. It was from these diaries that he published in 1887 the small book entitled *An Easter Vacation in Greece*, and an article on "The South of France and the Riviera" in *The Eagle*, a magazine supported by the members of St John's College, in the year 1882. From the latter we quote the following passage:

Thursday, Jan. 12. On our way (from Pegli to Spezia by train) we had many pleasant glimpses of the sea and the rocks and the sunset, with richly wooded hills to the east and far-extending valleys with the distant campanili of many a distant village. We reached our destination at about five o'clock and stayed at the Grand Hôtel de Spezia, a very comfortable house, where we had a capital room, with the Bay of Spezia, about seven miles long by three broad, in full view from our windows. The harbour is accurately described by Strabo as "one of the finest and largest in the world, containing within itself many minor ports, and surrounded by high mountains, with deep water close to the shore". It is far too faintly praised by Ennius, as quoted in the well-known lines of Persius:

> "mihi nunc Ligus ora
> intepet, hibernatque meum mare, qua latus ingens
> dant scopuli et multa litus se valle receptat.
> 'Lunai portum, est operae, cognoscite cives'.
> cor iubet hoc Enni". (VI. 9.)

In Silius Italicus (VIII, 483–5) we have a less familiar reference, which may be rendered as follows:

> "From Luna's mines of marble,
>   of marble white as snow,
> From Luna's famous harbour,
>   they throng to meet the foe.
> In all the world's great havens
>   none nobler can there be,
> Where barques beyond all number
>   might 'scape the stormy sea".

Friday, Jan. 13. We rose before sunrise while the moon was still shining on the Portus Lunae, and watched its light slowly paling in the dawn. Before us was the calm bay, with scarcely a ripple on its waters; beyond this, a long headland of rugged hills, over which the sun was soon to rise, and to the left, the loftier range of the Carrara mountains.

After breakfast, we made an excursion to the Porto Venere, a lovely little harbour to the west of the southern part of Spezia. To walk along the shore in front of the docks was impossible, and to have turned inland behind the arsenal would have in-

59

volved a tedious détour; so we took a small boat in the harbour and were rowed across part of the upper portion of the bay to a small village on its western shore called Murola, by an old boatman who told us in Italian that his name was Muscovia (?), and adroitly added that his father and his brother, both of whom were now dead, had known Lord Byron. On leaving the boat, we walked along the shore, and, after some little loss of time in finding the way, struck on the broad high-road which runs a little inland, commanding fine views of the harbour as it gradually ascends from point to point. After about an hour's walk, we came in full view of the Seno delle Grazie, a delightful little bay running inland between the Fort of Pezzino and the Punto di Lazaretto. Soon after, we passed a narrower breadth of blue water and reached the quiet bay of La Castagna, just beyond the long breakwater which extends across the mouth of the harbour of Spezia. A few minutes further brought us in sight of the bluest bay of all, that of the Porto Venere. Across its waters bright in the sunshine lay the large green island of Palmaria, famous in ancient times for its marble quarries, and now the happy place where the government of Italy in its paternal kindness sends the brigands which it captures. The prospect of being banished to so beautiful an island struck one as offering an almost undue encouragement to the profession of brigandage.

Returning a short way, we sat down for a while on a sunny hillside near the shade of some olive-trees, with thyme and myrtle around us, watching the eastern side of the great bay, with the road beneath us and olive-trees beyond it, and then a fort guarding the entrance to the bay, and the harbour-bar beyond. On the further side of the bar was another fort, and, to the south of the latter, the old castle of Lerici. Over this castle extended a range of broken hills of varying height; and, above all, a magnificent sweep of snow-clad summits stretching from north to south for the whole length of the view. In the outer part of the great harbour of Italy, an Italian man of war was moving to and fro and from time to time firing off cannons

60

whose echoes resounded far and wide in the hills that bound the bay; while all the blue breadth of water was brightened again and again by the white sails of many a boat that was speeding onward to the harbour.

After enjoying for a while the wider views of the bay of the Graces and the harbour of Porto Venere, which were to be seen from a level piece of ground above the place where we had rested, we came down to the road and walked along the hillside above Porto Venere, soon reaching the little village, which is called by the same name, with its lofty houses of many a varied hue rising from the very verge of the deep blue water. Passing some fishing boats near a small quay, we entered the village by a long and narrow archway, and went straight up a long, steep alley, which is the only street of the place. On emerging from this, and reaching the open rocks we had a good view of the island of Palmaria across a narrow strait, which forms the entrance to the little harbour; and, shortly afterwards, made our way up to the lonely ruins of San Pietro, an old church with alternate courses of black and white marble, built by the men of Pisa in 1118, marking the site of an ancient temple of Venus, which gave the harbour its name. Near this is found a peculiar variety of black marble streaked with bands of yellow, which is sold under the name of "Portor", being so called from the place where it is found. From the rocky ledges outside the ruined church, we had a magnificent view of the iron-bound coast outside the harbour and of all the shore between us and the lighthouse of Genoa. Below us was a small bay, girt with overhanging rocks, whose gloomy recesses are known to us as the Grotto of the Harpies. As we returned, some large fishing smacks came in full sail into the harbour of Porto Venere through the narrow strait between us and the island of Palmaria. It was here that Evelyn entered the port, according to the description which he gives us in his delightful diary:

"*October* 19*th*, 1644. We embarked in a felucca for Livorno, or Leghorn; but the sea running very high, we put in at Porto Venere, which we made with peril, between two narrow horrid

61

rocks, against which the sea dashed with great velocity; but we were soon delivered into as great a calm and a most ample harbour, being in the Golfo di Spetia".

At the little harbour we engaged a boatman to row us back to Spezia. On our way we saw the ruined fort of the Scola off the island of Palmaria, near a headland which goes by the somewhat incongruous name of Capo Smith, after an Englishman of that name who has, or had, a villa near it. We then passed between the breakwater and the western shore of the bay into the quieter waters of the harbour; and while the sun sank behind the hills, we enjoyed lovely and ever-varying views of the shores on both sides. As we drew near the quay, a small steamer shot past us, towing to land a large boatful of smart young Italian sailors.

In the course of the same tour Sandys visited and described in *The Eagle* the Roman amphitheatre at Nîmes, and the Roman aqueduct known as the Pont du Gard.

The natural pendant to this tour was a visit to the north of Italy in the Easter vacation of the following year, from Milan *via* Florence to Venice. The following extract, taken at random from the diary kept by Sandys, illustrates the variety of his interests:

March 22, 1883. (Ravenna.) Walked to the market place and looked at the pillars of the Hercules-basilica, a series of elegant Corinthian columns one or two of which bear what is sometimes considered the monogram of Theodoric.

Then down a narrow street to Dante's tomb. We were able to peer into the little shrine through the iron lattice of the doors; in front of the tomb lay a number of withered garlands and other memorials.

Next to the picture Gallery. Here are several casts of Canova's works, including one of his Endymion, which he did not live to execute. Also a bust of Thorwaldsen by himself.

Thence to the Library, where we saw the Ravenna MS. of Aristophanes and a MS. of Cicero's Letters including part of the first six books to Atticus; also a MS. of Dante's *Divina Commedia* written by his son. Among the modern books were treatises by Lubbock and Darwin translated into Italian.

Next to the Cathedral, where a special service was going on, attended by a large number of clergy, including the Bishop. Behind the altar, we saw the two large fragments of the ancient ambo of the 5th century bearing the name of Agnellus.

Then to the Baptistery, where we saw and admired the grand mosaics of the 5th century, with their rich blue background and bright golden hues.

Next to the church of San Vitale, where we sat down in the chapel behind the chief altar. Above us were the mosaics of Justinian and Theodora, besides numerous sacred subjects, clothing all the upper portions of the wall with an apparently imperishable beauty....

In the course of the next two years Mr and Mrs Sandys visited France, Belgium, Germany, Holland and the Channel Islands. And in 1886 they spent the Easter vacation in Greece.

The tour in Greece embraced Athens and Eleusis, the Argolid, Delphi and Olympia, Zacynthos and Corcyra. Although Sandys derived the greatest pleasure from this visit to the more important classical sites, the account of his experiences, which he published in the following year, is on the whole disappointing; this was mainly due to the fact that his knowledge of ancient Greece manifested itself in the form of a classical commentary which tended to obscure the charm of modern Greece. One of the most pleasant passages describes the ascent of Mt Pentelicus from the monastery Pentele, which lies beneath the mountain:

At the monastery there was some building going on, but we failed to find a monk to guide us to the summit. However, our

63

driver, who was a handsome young Greek with a well-bronzed complexion, got an intelligent quarryman, who was looking after some blocks of marble in front of the monastery, to show us the way. We began our walk about eleven o'clock, and after crossing some plantations on comparatively level ground, went steadily up the hill along paths that were strewn with shining fragments of marble, and across little lawns that were carpeted with bright anemones, till the flowers became fewer and fewer, and the ascent increasingly rugged. Toward the south-west, the familiar panorama of hills and islands began once more to disclose itself, and Salamis, Aegina, Epidaurus, and the mountains of the Morea came into fuller and fuller view. We paused for a while near the ancient quarries in front of a low cliff of solid marble, scored with the names of modern Greeks and Russians carved in massive characters. To our right was a large cavern with graceful festoons of maiden-hair and gleaming stalactites falling from its roof; and in its floor, in a square basin of marble, a small pool of clear cold water. Our guide was a quiet and unobtrusive companion, with a gentle and kindly politeness in all he did, and with an enviable power of sustained endurance in climbing up the roughest of paths. I followed him for a little way into the darker and cooler part of the cave, without caring to respond for long to his repeated invitation: πήγαινε κάτω πήγαινε κάτω ("Come down!"). To the right, just outside the cave, was a small chapel carved out of the rock with a shrine fitted up with an altar, and a ceiling decorated with Byzantine frescoes. This was about half-way. After struggling on over blocks of stone and branches of stunted brushwood, we reached a point of outlook from which we had our first view of Euboea, with its rugged hills rising beyond the narrow straits. From the same point we looked down for the first time on the battlefield of Marathon, bounded on the land-side by its fringe of low hills, with the road to Athens running between them and closed toward the shore by the crescent shaped bay, familiar in all the maps and plans of the battle. The battlefield, in the words of Byron, "preserves alike its bounds and boundless fame".

On reaching the summit, 3640 feet above the sea, we sheltered ourselves from the cold blast behind some rude stone walls, and enjoyed the full magnificence of the panorama. To the north was the finest point of all, the snowy pyramid of Mount Dirphys in Euboea rising to the height of more than 5000 feet. Towards the south and south-east, among the many islands now in sight, were several of the Cyclades, Andros, Tenos, and Ceos, with some of the smaller islands off the Cape of Sunium, which was itself hidden from view by the hills of the mining district of Laurium; while to the north-west, among the villages of Attica, we saw close at hand the hamlet of Tatoi near the famous fort of Decelea, which guarded the most eastern of the passes of Parnes. Immediately below us to the north, we looked down once more on the field of Marathon. According to Pausanias (i. 32. 2), there was a statue of Athene on Pentelicus, probably on the actual summit; and it can hardly be doubted that it was from the crest of this very mountain that the gleaming shield was lifted up, which was supposed to have been displayed by the Alcmaeonidae as a signal to the Persians immediately after the battle (Herodotus, VI. 115).

At 2.30 we began to descend, and at about 4.30 reached the menastery, having taken about five hours in all. After an *al fresco* lunch rather late in the day, we started back at 5 o'clock, and found the anemones, which had looked so bright as we came, already closing their petals for the night. The strong cold wind of the morning had given way to a warmer air, while we watched the sun descending in a sky of pale amber behind the delicately purple hills as we returned to Athens.

The knowledge of modern Greece, which he acquired during this tour, was the more valuable to Sandys, because in 1883 he had acceded to the request to become a member of the Executive Committee for the establishment of a British School of Archaeological and Classical Studies at Athens. The initial proposal for the foundation of the School was voiced by Sir Richard Jebb in his "Plea for a British Institute at Athens"; at a meeting, convened by the Prince of Wales and attended by Mr Gladstone and other distinguished public men, the Executive Committee was formed to carry the proposal into effect. Sandys gave loyal and strong support to Sir Richard Jebb in the foundation of the School and in the difficult early period of its existence, and for many years he represented its interests in Cambridge University. When his health began to break, Sir John was compelled to resign the position of Cambridge representative on the Managing Committee of the British School. Shortly after his resignation, the then Director of the British School, Mr A. J. B. Wace, in a letter concerning the funds for the excavations at Mycenae, writes:

We are very sorry to hear that reasons of health have compelled you to resign your place as the Cambridge Representative on the Managing Committee. May I seize the opportunity to express to you in the name of the School and its students our heartiest thanks for your long and devoted service to the interests of the School. We feel that we are losing in you an old and well-tried friend.

During the years 1887–1900 Sandys, accompanied by Mrs Sandys, made many tours in Europe, ranging from Constantinople to Scotland and including the Cyclades, Sicily and the Channel Islands. In the August of 1892 he attended the Wagner Festival at Bayreuth, and heard four operas, *Tannhäuser*, *Die Meistersinger*, *Tristan und Isolde*, and *Parsifal*; though not himself a performer, he was very appreciative of classical music, and was for some years President of the St John's College Musical

66

Society. He attended the Jubilee celebration of the Cambridge University Musical Society in 1893, and listened to the four famous composers, who participated in the concert and who were to be presented for honorary degrees on the following day, Herr Max Bruch, M. Saint-Saëns, Signor Boito, and M. Tschaikowsky. He also saw the Passion Play at Oberammergau in 1890.

During his travels in Europe, he was especially attached to Italy, though he often revisited the Riviera, Normandy and Germany. He and Mrs Sandys spent the Easter vacation of 1889 in Sicily, where they visited many classical sites; this tour, like that undertaken in Greece, was always remembered by him as particularly enjoyable, for he drew from it a meed of pleasure, such as is only possible to one steeped in the literature of Greece and Rome. At Syracuse he traced the course of the great siege by Athens and followed the River Anapus to its source; visited the temples of Agrigentum, Segesta and Selinus, and tried to discover a specimen of that elusive plant, the ancient σέλινον; climbed up to the lofty city of Enna, and admired the bay of Palermo. He also undertook the ascent of Mt Eryx, which he describes in his diary:

Took the train to Trapani, where we started at once to walk up Mount Eryx, about 700 metres high, taking on our way the church of the Annunziata which lies half an hour outside the town. Soon after this we began our ascent by a rugged mule-path, the wind blowing in violent and sudden blasts most of the time. During our climb we descried not far from the shore to the north the wave-washed reef of the island (of Asinello), which according to Virgil's narrative was the spot where Aeneas planted the ilex-branch as a goal for the galleys in the race, during the funeral games in honour of Anchises (Aen. v. 124 f.). As we continued our ascent we had lovely views of blue bays and of the Aegates insulae, three of which were particularly prominent with their rocky masses towards the west of Trapani, the outlines of which recalled the ancient name of δρέπανον.

Near the summit we entered the mist and began to wonder how far we might be from the village, which crowns the crest, when we suddenly found ourselves in front of massive walls and a vast portal, beyond which we met some kindly people clad in blue cloaks with the hoods thrown over their heads. They took us to see their principal church, which is remarkably fine for its secluded situation. We had no time to see any more, as we had taken about two hours and a half, and the train had to be caught for our return to Marsala. As the rain came on with some violence soon after, we hastened down and overtook the post and drove down to the railway station instead of walking.

His description of his first day at Syracuse is also interesting; it illustrates the energy with which Mr and Mrs Sandys habitually carried out their tours, and his description of the railway journey to Syracuse demonstrates once more the alertness of his powers of observation, where classical history was concerned.

April 3. Rose early and started at 4.50 for Syracuse. The journey along the coast was particularly interesting. During the early part of it we were crossing the most fertile tract in Sicily, the plano di Catania, the fields of the Laestrygones, described by Cicero as uberrima Siciliae pars; near passo Martino we crossed the Simeto (the ancient Symaethus), a stream of no great breadth, which with its tributaries drains a seventh part of Sicily. Then through a more hilly district past the Lago di Lentini, the largest piece of water in Sicily but nonexistent in ancient times. It derives its name from the small town of Lentini, the ancient Leontini, one of the oldest Greek settlements in Sicily, founded in 729 at the same time as Catana. It is also well known as the birthplace of Gorgias (483–376), who was sent as an envoy to Athens in 427. Returning to the coast, we passed along the shore of the bay of Megara, where the ruins of Megara Hyblaea lie between two streams of the Alcantares and the S. Gusmano. The honey of Hybla came from the flowery slopes to our right, where the small town of Mellili now stands.

As we came nearer to Syracuse, our train passed along the small bay of Trogilus, and keeping to the coast near Achradina, reached the station at eight in the morning. During the journey we had several fine views of Etna.

Stayed at the Casa Politi (room no. 2, in the new part of our hotel, overlooking the Great Harbour). Walked from the modern Syracuse (which, like the ancient settlement, is confined to the island of Ortygia) to the Latomia dei Capuccini, a vast deserted quarry rich with vegetation. Wandered about the southern ledge of Epipolae and returned to the hotel.

In the afternoon drove to Euryalus by the road south of Epipolae. Walked about the vast galleries below the fort and went into several of the places supposed to have been used for storing water; near the entrance of each of these some Phoenician characters were to be seen deeply carved in the rock. Enjoyed the view of the Harbour from the top of the rocks above the Fort, with the Belvedere lying further inland, a prominent height, sometimes identified as Euryalus. Having dismissed our carriage, we walked back along a path beneath the walls of Dionysius, under olive-trees with beautiful glimpses of the sea towards Thapsus. Ascended Epipolae once more by the old road at a point called the Scala della Targetta, and walked along a cross road running West to East and connecting the road by which we had reached the ridge with the broad road from Catania. Walked along the latter across what was nearly the broadest part of the plateau and so returned rather late for dinner.

The last of the tours, of which Sandys kept a diary, was in Algeria, where he visited Tunis and Batna to see Carthage and Timgad. At the beginning of the diary

69

are summarised some of the descriptions of earlier travellers in this district, who interested themselves in the classical topography and remains. On this tour, as in those in Greece and Sicily, Sandys was naturally interested chiefly in the classical associations of the places which he visited, but his diary also reflects his interest in the invasions of the Arabs. In Algeria he and Mrs Sandys travelled from Tunis to Algiers *via* Constantine, Biskra and Kharata; they visited many classical sites and Sandys copied numerous inscriptions in places not often visited. His descriptions of Carthage and Timgad are interesting in themselves:

17 *March* 1894. Drove to Carthage, along the north shore of the lake of Tunis. During a large part of the drive asphodels and anemones were to be seen brightening the waste ground along the roadside. Drove first to La Marsa and saw the exterior of the palace of the Bey and that of the Cardinal Lavigerie. Near the latter had our lunch by the side of an olive-yard reminding us of days in Greece and on the Riviera. Thence to Sidi Bon-Said, a native village with its cluster of white houses set on the highest part of Cape Carthage. From the Phare enjoyed the view extending from the Cape of Apollo in the north-west to the Cape of Mercury in the south-east. Then to the cisterns of Punic origin, now restored and still used for the supply of water in the region of the Golatta. Next to the hill of Byrsa where we visited the Museum with its numerous Punic and Carthaginian inscriptions, and its vast collection of ancient lamps and coins, besides mosaics and terracottas. Many of the epitaphs and fragments of sculpture are let into the plaster on the inner surface of the wall enclosing the garden in front of the Museum. In the centre of the garden is the Chapel of St Louis with the epitaph in memory of the French Consul who secured the site for the chapel.

From the citadel we enjoyed a view of the harbour of Carthage, the nearer harbour which is of a circular shape and has a circular island in the middle, and the further harbour which is rectangular in form.

On driving back, we saw some of the sites of the ancient tombs and walked past some of the ancient cisterns, now turned into dwelling-places, or used for keeping animals in them, by the people of Malga. Near the railway station visited the remains of the Amphitheatre in which Perpetua was martyred. A most interesting day altogether: our drive began shortly after 10 and ended after 6 o'clock.

April 4. At 8.15 in the morning started on our drive to Timgad, thirty-six kilometres east of Batna. The drive there was more enjoyable as the day was bright and sunny, and the air exhilarating. We were more than three thousand feet above sea level, and the mountains of the Dures range were in many cases crowned with snow. Our route went through Lambessa, which we had visited on the previous day. During the whole day there was not a tree to be seen along our route: only a few shrubs near Lambessa. Toward the end of our drive, which lasted nearly four hours, we had to cross some muddy streams, the driver making his horses rush down into them and up the steep bank on the opposite side, a course attended with a considerable amount of splashing.

On arrival we were met by the Arab guide who conducted us to the various objects of interest.

From the Triumphal Arch, which lies to the north-west of the principal buildings of the town and spans the Roman road, which makes an obtuse angle at this point in its course from Setif and Lambessa to Tebessa and Constantine (Cirta). On both sides of this road, to the east of the arch, runs a colonnade: many of the pillars of which are still standing. As one passes along these pillars on the south side of the road, one sees the remains of a series of shops with the letters VIPII or VIPIIDII deeply incised on the upright stones to the right of the entrance. In this row of shops there was a fountain of water and in front of it a short inscription running in two lines, not far above the pavement of the road.

Turning to the right from the Roman road we reached the remains of the Forum, which measures 49·30 metres by 44·30, and is entirely paved. Here there are numerous inscriptions; amongst others one in honour of Volontius Pudens Pomponianus (quoted by Playfair p. 210 a). On the west of the Forum is the elevated platform for public harangues; on the right and left of this are two inscriptions on pedestals of white marble, both beginning with the words VICTORIAE PARTHICAE AUG. SACR., and both commemorating the victories of Trajan over the Parthians. The 30th legion is here mentioned as the Legio Ulpia Victrix, and it has been inferred that the veterans of this legion were rewarded by Trajan by being established at Thamugas. Immediately to the east of the Forum is the Basilica, and behind this (to the east) the Latrinae Publicae, the general plan of which is semicircular with the position of the feet in each partition clearly marked and with a space for a narrow stream of water scooped out of the marble floor.

After lunch near the Arch, we surveyed the ruins for a second time—this time unattended by the guide—and made our way to the main square building to the south, known as the Byzantine Fort by Salomon, the lieutenant of Belisarius.

Some memoranda of the inscriptions which I noticed in various parts of the ruins, as well as the more recent discoveries, which include a fountain near the theatre, and a large part of the Thermae (with the hypocaust) are entered in pencil at the end of this book.

We spent nearly four hours at the ruins which are most interesting, forming the nearest approach to Pompeii that I have ever seen. The most thrilling feature is the Triumphal Arch and the Roman road.

The drive back took nearly three hours and the whole day was most enjoyable, the day bright and sunny, and the air bracing since Batna lies more than three thousand feet above the level of the sea.

It is clear from these citations that Sandys travelled like Herodotus ἱστορίης ἕνεκεν, for, wherever his travels led him, he was possessed by the spirit of keen and critical inquiry, which did not however limit his power of appreciation. The wide range of interests which we have noticed in his diaries reflects the distinguishing characteristic of his scholarship—a comprehensive knowledge of all departments of classical studies and an enthusiastic interest in any modern discoveries. Apart from the influence which this use of his leisure exerted on the training and refreshing of his mind, his travels had a direct effect on his published work.

One of the last books, if not the last, which he read before his death, was a French work on the history of Arles. The taste for modern and mediaeval history, which he retained throughout his life, was born during his Repton days and developed by the knowledge which was made accessible to him through travel; and it was this interest and knowledge of mediaeval times which inspired and strengthened his greatest work, the *History of Classical Scholarship*. At the same time we have seen that in his editions of texts he made full use of Continental scholarship and added illustrations of manuscripts and monuments which he had consulted abroad. As Public Orator, he often presented for degrees eminent foreigners, and with many of these he contracted friendships; he also frequently attended public functions at Continental Universities, on one occasion the centenary celebrations at Halle University, when he stayed with his old friend, Professor Blass. His unfailing courtesy and kindness won him the affection of many visitors to

Cambridge; among his letters is the following from Herr Cramer:

I have still to thank you for the very kind letter and the copy of College rules you sent me on to Freiburg last year.

Now I want to ask you another favour to-day. Would you be able to find out the address of Mr Wilson, whose rooms I kept during my stay at Cambridge? The reason, why I would know it, is this. When Mr Wilson returned home at the end of the term, he was in want of his new gown for some reason. In spite of our making an exact search we could not find out, where it had remained. It was only some time after my having left England, when I remembered that some day quite in the beginning there came a student, who went to the chest of drawers and took out Mr Wilson's gown. As I believed him to be a friend of Mr Wilson's I did not object at his doing so, nor did I attach any importance to the matter. It appears that the gown was never returned and I feel somewhat uneasy about it, having learned in the course of time more exactly the responsibility of man in such cases. Now I would like to clear myself of the matter by offering to Mr Wilson an indemnification....

What further steps were taken in the matter, is not recorded, but no doubt the unhappiness of this victim of undergraduate habits was duly alleviated.

Of Sandys' friendly relations with foreign scholars the following letter affords an example:

Göttingen, Friedlander Weg 35, *d.* 1sten *Juni* 1897.

Hochgeehrter Herr!

Gestern empfing ich Ihre Sendung mit den Collationen der beiden Harpocration Handschriften; ich habe sie sofort durchgesehen und kann Ihnen nun von Herzen danken für die aufopfernde Liebenswürdigkeit, mit der Sie meine unbescheidenen Wünsche erfüllt haben. Sie haben mir dadurch eine wertvolle Dienst erwiesen: ich werde über die Stellung der beiden Codices

74

nun sicher urteilen können. Es wird mir ein besonderes Vergnugen sein, Ihnen die Ausgabe der Rednerlexikon zu überreichen. Heute erlaube ich mir zwei Publicationen von mir an Sie abgehen zu lassen und bitte, wenn Sie sie ansehen, daran zu denken, dass ihr Verfasser sich Ihrer in Dankbarkeit erinnert.. . .

Nicht minder dankbar bin ich Ihnen für die Notizen über das Lex. Cant. und vor allen Dingen auch für Ihr liebenswürdiger Anerbieten, die Handschrift zu vergleichen. Ich werde die Bearbeitung des Lexicon in diesen Tagen in Angriff nehmen und sehen, ob eine völlige Nachvergleichung nötig wird, hoffe aber, Ihre Güte nur für ein paar zweifelhafte Stellen in Anspruch zu nehmen.

Genehmigen Sie den Ausdruck der dankbaren Ergebenheit und der angezeichneten Hochachtung

Ihres

G. WENTZEL.

In 1900 Sandys was fifty-six years of age and he began to feel the strain of combining so many offices; moreover it had become increasingly important that he should devote as much time as possible to his own work. He therefore did not seek re-election to the Tutorship at St John's College, which he had held for thirty years; the conscientious thoroughness, with which he had executed the difficult duties of this office for so long a period, had won him the respect and admiration of his colleagues, and the grateful friendship of a generation of pupils. He continued to serve the College, of which he was so proud, with the same loyalty as a College Lecturer for the next nine years and as a member of the Governing Body for most of the remainder of his life. On New Year's Day, 1900, just before his resignation, he began to work on the subject, which was to claim much of his time for the next eight years, the *History of Classical Scholarship*.

75

Before concluding this period of Sandys' life, we must mention that Sandys stood as a candidate for the Professorship of Greek at Edinburgh University in 1882, vacated by Professor Blackie. Although Sandys was not in fact elected, the testimonials which he obtained bear witness to his prominence among Cambridge scholars. We quote some of them here, because they emphasise the peculiar qualities of Sandys' work during these twenty years. There are testimonials from thirty eminent scholars, among whom we may mention B. H. Kennedy, W. H. Thompson, J. E. B. Mayor, A. S. Wilkins, C. Waldstein, W. Sanday, F. A. Paley, J. P. Mahaffy, E. A. Abbott, J. S. Reid, F. Blass, A. Schaefer, A. Michaelis and N. Wecklein.

From the Rev. John E. B. Mayor, Professor of Latin in the University of Cambridge, and formerly Librarian of the University, Editor of Juvenal, etc., etc.

Mr Sandys attended my lectures as an undergraduate, and has been repeatedly examined by me. For several years he was my colleague as a lecturer in College, and of late years, as Public Orator of the University, has been associated with me in the examinations for the University Scholarships and the Chancellor's Classical Medals. I have also read carefully all that he has publi.hed.

I never had a pupil more thoroughly conscientious in his work; year by year his services to classical scholarship have been increasing. Not merely as a teacher on the old lines, but as a reformer and introducer of new methods and new branches of study, his influence has made itself felt. It was an arduous task to succeed Professor Jebb as Orator; by universal consent Mr Sandys fully maintains the fame of a post which has been filled by some of the greatest Cambridge scholars; his speeches are models of terse and felicitous description. His published works include editions of Attic orators, of the *Bacchae* of Euri-

76

pides, and of the *Rhetoric* of Aristotle. The Commentary of Mr Cope on the last of these having been left imperfect, the authorities of Trinity College selected Mr Sandys, then very young and of a rival house, to digest and complete Mr Cope's collections.

Mr Sandys is also widely read in the best English and foreign Literature, and has devoted special attention to Archaeology, a subject which has hitherto been much neglected here.

As Tutor of this College for several years, under very difficult circumstances, he has shown great tact and determination. He not only made friends of his pupils during residence, but keeps up an acquaintance with them in after life, such as would be impossible to any but a man of methodical and orderly habits.

I can best estimate Edinburgh University's gain, if it appoints Mr Sandys to the Chair vacated by Professor Blackie, by thinking of the loss which his departure would bring upon Cambridge and upon his College,—a loss which, so far as I can see, at the present juncture would be irreparable.

From A. S. Wilkins, Professor of Latin and Comparative Philology in the Victoria University, Manchester.

...I would especially direct attention to the completeness of his literary work. Even among scholars of high rank it is often found that there is on the one hand an ignorance of the latest results of German learning and research, or on the other an absence of the finished elegance and accuracy which marks the best British Scholarship. In both respects Mr Sandys' productions have always appeared to me alike admirable.

From C. Waldstein, Lecturer on Classical Archaeology in the University of Cambridge.

Nothing I believe is more wanted in a professor of Greek than that he should be many-sided in his interests and bring real life into the study of the Greek past in appreciating and depicting ancient life in all its aspects. I believe that a teacher of Greek Literature has only partly grasped the spirit of his own subject

77

if he is not appreciative of the other manifestations of the Greek people's genius, their art. Now, it is this side which I have always noticed in you, and which has often encouraged me in my endeavours to advance the study of Archaeology here. But you have manifested this breadth of interest not only by word and deed, but also in your published works. The best testimony of this is your edition of the *Bacchae* of Euripides in which, for the first time, you added life to an ancient author in introducing considerations and actual illustrations of an archaeological nature. I hope your example will be followed by others.

CHAPTER V

1900   1914

THE main reason for Sandys' resignation of the Tutorship at St John's College was that the heavy duties involved in that office interfered with his scholastic output; the wisdom of this course was fully proved by the remarkable productivity of the remaining years of his life. Moreover it is to these last years that his most distinguished work is assigned—a remarkable proof of his mental vitality and enthusiasm. For, while his editions of classical authors had gained him a reputation equalled only by a few leading contemporary scholars, his *History of Classical Scholarship* was so far in advance of the earlier works on this subject that its position was unique; further, the treatment of the subject was such that its appeal was not limited to students of the classics but embraced all who were interested in the history of Humanism. The compilation of this work entailed wide research into virgin fields of classical studies; for, in addition to the fact that no comprehensive book had ever before been written on the history of classical scholarship, the few monographs on the subject were highly specialised and in many cases out of date. It is indeed a singular proof of Sandys' facility for working at high speed that the third volume of this encyclopaedic study was published only eight years after the work was planned in 1900, and that despite the other claims on his time during these years.

More than all his other works the *History of Classical*

Scholarship is representative of Sandys' interests and talents. We have already had reason to remark on his knowledge of mediaeval and modern history; here it was admirably applied. The scope of his travels had enabled him to consult personally the manuscripts and early works of classical scholars, and equipped him with a full understanding of national temperaments and national ideals in scholarship; his acquaintance with classical Byzantine and mediaeval art enriched his understanding of the cultural aims of these periods. A profound believer in the importance of classical studies and in the value of tradition, he pursued his subject with a deep-seated enthusiasm and infused his writing with a living spirit; moreover, it had always been his aim to widen the circle of interest in the classics and to trace its influence upon the art and letters of the modern world—an ever-present necessity for the vitality of classical studies—and in the *History of Classical Scholarship* this aim was strikingly effected.

A more specific preparation for this work can be seen in the research into mediaeval manuscripts which had often accompanied Sandys' editions of separate texts. In 1896 he delivered a series of lectures in Cambridge, taking as his subject " The History of Classical Learning in England ". He first began to work on the history of scholarship in 1897 when he was asked to contribute to the *Companion to Greek Studies*, edited by Mr Whibley in 1905, with a chapter on the "History of Greek Scholarship". On January 1, 1900, shortly before he resigned his Tutorship, he started to work on the *History of Classical Scholarship*, bringing to bear on the subject the full power of a mature and experienced judgment.

The first volume appeared in 1903 and reached a second edition as early as 1906, while the second and third volumes were published in 1908. They were received with unstinted approbation at the time, nor has their reputation diminished with the growth of a new generation of Cambridge scholars. We may quote from notices which appeared in *The Times* and *The Spectator*:

A monument of compressed information, sound scholarship, and solid learning. It is, in short, exactly what such a book should be, avoiding controversy, imparting information, and at the same time so pleasantly written as to carry the reader smoothly along from one stage of his journey to another.... Dr Sandys never loses himself in details, nor forgets in following out its ramifications the main object of his work. There is nothing of the kind, so far as we know, in English literature, and the work has been so thoroughly done that it is not likely to be superseded. It does honour to Cambridge, and, indeed, to England, so comprehensive is it in its scope, and so rich and varied in its treatment of the subject.

To venture on an almost untrodden field, to explore the obscure annals "of twenty-five centuries", and not only to set forth the facts with scrupulous accuracy and absolute clearness, but also to estimate them with a critical and just judgment— this is a task from which most men would have shrunk, but which Dr Sandys has achieved. To praise his work is needless, for the earlier portion of it has already received full and final approval. It is a work which will last, and in this noble tribute to the dead scholars of the past he has set up his own enduring memorial.

And from *The Times Literary Supplement* of January 29, 1904:

It is no light task to write the history of classical scholarship.

It requires ripe scholarship in the historian, a wide grasp of the history of European literature, a keen sympathy alike with learning, letters, and thought, a vigilant sense of proportion, a trained critical faculty, and no ordinary gift of literary presentation to prevent the survey of so vast a subject from degenerating into a bald enumeration of names, dates, and titles. For classical scholarship is, in truth, the substratum of all European literature. Dig into the latter where we will, we find, if we only dig deep enough, that it has its origins and its roots in the thought of classical Hellas. The history of classical scholarship is therefore in a sense the history of European culture. But in order to render such a subject tractable to the historian it must be taken in a somewhat narrower sense. Classical scholarship is taken by Dr Sandys as meaning "the accurate study of the language, literature, and art of Greece and Rome, and of all that they teach us as to the nature and history of man". Even so he has undertaken a gigantic task, one which involves a survey of all Greek and Roman literature and of all their derivative streams in theology, philosophy, and *belles lettres* extending in time over some twenty-five centuries, and in space, let us say, from Caesarea to Seville, from Upsala to the Thebaid. Such tasks are not often attempted in these days of specialism. A Morhof with his *Polyhistor*, or a Hoffman with his *Lexicon Universale* may seem to take all previous knowledge for his province, a Bayle may produce a *Dictionnaire Historique et Critique* not more remarkable for what it contains than for what it omits, but modern scholars are either more modest or more minute. They approximate rather to the scarabeist than to the entomologist, to borrow the distinction of the *Autocrat of the Breakfast Table*, and rarely aspire to complete the circle of knowledge, even of the knowledge of classical antiquity and all that it has meant for the ages. But Dr Sandys is of the heroic race, one of those students of whom Matthew Arnold speaks as "of the force of Wolff, who used to sit up the whole night with his feet in a tub of cold water and one of his hands bound up while he read with the other, and who thus managed to get through all the Greek and Latin classics at school, and also Scapula's Lexicon and Faber's Thesaurus; and who at Göttingen would sweep clean out of the library shelves all the books illustrative of the classic which Heyne was going to lecture on, and finish them in a week. Such students", continues Matthew Arnold, "are rare, and nine out of ten, especially in England where much time is given to Greek and Latin composition, never get through the philological vestibule at all, never arrive at *Altertumswissenschaft* which is a knowledge of the spirit and power of Greek and Roman antiquities learned from its original works ". That Dr Sandys has given much time to Latin composition at least, his graceful utterances as Public Orator at Cambridge are on record to show; but he at any rate has not halted too long in the philological vestibule, for his very definition of classical scholarship is a testimony to the spirit and power of Greek and Roman antiquity, and his treatment of its history is a proof that he has arrived at *Altertumswissenschaft* and at a great deal else besides....

On the Continent and in America the great value of Sandys' work was at once recognised; in Germany especially his appreciation of German scholarship was warmly praised, and the comprehensive nature of the *History* established his reputation above that of contemporary English scholars. We read in the *Literarisches Zentralblatt* of June 26, 1909:

Die Vorzüge, die Blass dem ersten Band nachgerühmt hat, eignen in gleicher Weise den beiden vorliegenden. Hervorzuheben ist namentlich die gründliche Sachkenntnis, die allenthalben hervortritt, und die klare, geschmackvolle Form, die die Lektüre des Buches überaus genussreich macht. Die Darstellung selbst besteht zum grössten Teil aus biographischen Einzelporträts....Die Porträts, die der Verfasser von den Meistern unserer Wissenschaft entwirft, sind im ganzen trefflich gelungen. In der Regel verfährt er so, dass er nach einer kurzen Skizze des äusseren Lebensganges die Hauptwerke der behandelten Persönlichkeiten bespricht, um hierbei und im Anschluss hieran ihre Eigenart und ihre Bedeutung für die Entwickelung der Philologie ins Relief zu setzen. Überaus dankenswert sind die tabellarischen Übersichten, die sich an geeigneten Stellen eingefügt finden. Einen erlesenen Schmuck der beiden Bände bilden die zahlreichen schönen Illustrationen, die uns eine ganze Anzahl unserer Grossen vor Augen führen. Mit besonderer Liebe und Ausführlichkeit hat Sandys die klassische Altertumswissenschaft im 19. Jahrh. dargestellt, ihr ist fast der ganze dritte Band gewidmet.... Uneingeschrankte Bewunderung verdient der Fleiss und die Gewissenhaftigkeit, mit der Sandys diese Aufgabe gelöst hat. Gewaltig ist der Umfang der von ihm beigezogenen und, wie genauere Nachprüfung jeden überzeugen wird, sorgsam ausgebeuteten Literatur. Dass einzelnes dem Spürsinn der gelehrten Verf. entgangen ist, kann bei der ungeheuren Ausdehnung des bebauten Feldes nicht wundernehmen.... Sandys' Buch, das Hauptwerk über den Gegenstand und gewiss auf lange der eigentliche Führer auf dem behandelten Gebiet. Wir wünschen dem gelehrten Verf. von Herzen Glück zur Vollendung seines mühsamen, überaus verdienstlichen Unternehmens. Er hat die philologische Literatur um ein standard work bereichert.

The portraits of distinguished scholars referred to in this review were collected carefully by Sandys. In his correspondence we find that he secured the purchase of a portrait of J. E. B. Mayor, and he also obtained a hitherto unpublished sketch of Mommsen. In the latter case he corresponded with his friend Wilamowitz-Möllendorff, who in his reply speaks warmly of the *History*:

7.iii.06.   *Westend-Berlin Eichenallée* 12.
Hochgeehrter Herr,
    Auf Ihren freundlichen Brief und die Anfrage über ein Porträt von Mommsen ist es mir eine Freude zu antworten: denn nach meinem Urteil ist das einzige würdige Porträt

Mommsens das eines Engländers, keine Photographie sondern eine Zeichnung von W. Richmond, die vervielfältigt und auch im Handel ist. Sie stammt aus dem Jahre 1890, zeigt also noch nicht dem Greis, dessen Äusseres sich zuletzt stark verändert hatte, und wenn die Angehörigen daher bei den Bildern bleiben, die ihnen die letzten Eindrücke erhalten, so kommt das für die Welt nicht in Betracht, die ihren Mommsen haben soll: es würde mir eine Freude sein, wenn Sie es wünschen, Ihnen diese Zeichnung zu übersenden....

Es ist mir eine Freude, dass Sie die Geschichte der Philologie über die Alteren Zeiten herab verfolgen. Unsere Wissenschaft hat Grund zur Pietät, gerade weil wir in anderen Geleisen fahren als selbst die grossen Philologen um Porson und Hermann. Ich kenne aber keine Darstellung, die von ferne genügte, und es liegt mir daran: ich habe eben Geschichte der Philologie gelesen.

Mit der Versicherung der vorzüglichsten Hochachtung Ihr sehr ergebner

U. WILAMOWITZ-MÖLLENDORFF.

In Italy the History of Renaissance Scholarship aroused a special interest: of many reviews we may quote from the philologist Carlo Pascal, writing in the *Bollettino di Filologia Classica*:

Abbiamo qui un' opera che abbraccia un immenso disegno: parecchi secoli di vita intellettuale, la storia a grandi tratti della critica letteraria é della filologia dalla più remota antichità sino alla fine del Medio Evo. A cagione della vastità della trattazione è naturale che l' autore non possa procedere se non per brevi accenni, rimandando nelle note ai lavori speciali chi desideri sui singoli argomenti più particolari informazioni. Quindi è che, anche quando l' opera assume una forma quasi di catalogo e non fa che enumerare fuggevolmente gli autori e gli scritti loro, essa è sempre utile, perchè fornisce le indicazioni necessarie per ricerche più profonde. Si tratta del resto di percorrere quasi venti secoli di attività critica e letteraria; e ciascuno può comprendere che l' autore di un tal prontuario deve dominare una immensa materia di studii critici antichi e moderni e dominarla in tal modo da portare i risultati più autorevoli e recenti e da serbare una equa proporzione tra le varie parti. Diamo lode al Sandys di essere riuscito molto bene nel difficile assunto.

It is characteristic of Sandys that he always made a point of sending presentation copies of his work to his friends, for his kindliness delighted to manifest itself in a thoughtful and courteous manner. Many of his pupils speak with gratitude of such gifts, and he always valued any suggestion or criticism that they might make. Of letters expressing thanks for such gifts we may quote a letter from the late Rector of Lincoln College, Oxford, which also alludes to Sandys' industry.

Lincoln College, Oxford.   13 *Nov.* 1906.

My dear Public Orator,

During the stress of work of my Vice-Chancellorship, I used to say to myself: "When I have a little leisure, I shall buy Sandys' *History of Scholarship*, and delight myself with reading it"! It is therefore a remarkable coincidence that just as I had laid down my burden and disposed of my arrears, your kind present of the volume came in the very nick of time to save you from one additional purchaser!

I hope you will set against that the real pleasure you have given me by your gift. I have begun the reading with great interest, and I am quite aghast at the amount of work and research you have condensed into so handy a book without making it anything but very readable.

I feel in a hurry to get to the latter part, as there I shall be in the happy condition—ὅτ᾽ ἀκήρατος ἦν ἔτι λειμών—and I feel how very much I have to learn about later scholars.

I have been having a curate-orator during my year of office as V.-C.; and now I am back at my old duty—tant bien que mal.

86

The duties of the Cambridge Orator are infinitely more diversified than those of his Oxford brother and this fills me with more amaze, when I think how much time you have been able to devote to your own studies.

Again let me thank you for your friendliness.

With kind regards,
Sincerely yours,

W. W. MERRY.

There is also a letter from Professor Gudeman, who was at that time engaged upon a second edition of his *Outlines of the History of Classical Philology*, thanking Sandys for the gift of his second edition of the first volume of the *History of Classical Scholarship*; he comments there on the reception of Sandys' work by the public: " It must be a source of gratification not only to you but to classical scholars generally that in these antihumanistic days a book such as yours has met with a great success ". The value of Sandys' work is justly assessed in a letter from the then Vice-Chancellor of Oxford.

Magdalen College, Oxford. November 16th, 1906.

My dear Dr Sandys,

You will excuse I know my writing by dictation, the only way in which a Vice-Chancellor can keep up with his letters and the only way in which I can tell you at all adequately how very much pleased I was to receive the other day your very kind gift of the second edition of your *History of Classical Scholarship*. I was pleased to get it may I say, first of all as a tribute to my office, and if I may venture to think and say so, a very pretty compliment from the Public Orator of the sister University. I was pleased also to receive it as the gift of one whom I would consider now an old friend and to whom more particularly since the loss of my dear friend Jebb at Cambridge I should naturally turn from time to time. But I was also pleased to have it for its own sake. I am delighted to think that it has got so quickly to a second edition. It is creditable to the book itself, but I think it is still more creditable to the public that they should have found out so rapidly its real value. The fact is that such books are very seldom indeed written with so much artistic and literary gift combined with so much business-like and practical arrangement. When I think how in my early days as a young fellow and scholar I used to pick out scraps here and there from heavy German and Latin treatises of the notes and comments of scattered scholars dealing with individual authors, I cannot but feel the contrast of the position which the young scholar finds himself in to-day thanks to this book of yours. You have made the whole history of scholarship, from Aristophanes of Athens as well as of Aristophanes of Byzantium (a very different person) down to our own day, a real and intelligible whole and I do not know which I enjoy or admire more, the treatment of the ancient or the mediaeval times. May I add one more word about the literary quality of the translations with which the book abounds? I know something of what is implied in these by having at times attempted them myself.

Believe me to be, with kind regards,
Yours sincerely,

T. HERBERT WARREN,
Vice-Chancellor.

In the interval between the appearance of the first volume of the *History of Classical Scholarship* and that of the second, Sandys delivered the Lane Lectures at Harvard University in 1905; this lectureship was established in memory of Professor Gardiner Martin Lane, a distinguished classical scholar, and Sandys' subject, "The Revival of Learning in Italy", was appropriate to the purpose of the foundation. As Public Orator, Sandys had presented many American scholars for honorary degrees, and on his visit to the United States he was most hospitably entertained by many of the most distinguished scholars of that time. In the course of his lectures he referred with great felicity to the close bond uniting the Old and the New Cambridge, and he paid a graceful tribute to American scholarship by mentioning the notable Latin orations delivered in old Cambridge in honour of Edward Everett, John Lothrop Motley, Robert C. Winthrop, Henry Wadsworth Longfellow, and James Russell Lowell, and the scarcely less distinguished addresses in English to Professor Cooke, Asa Gray, Oliver Wendell Holmes, Charles Eliot Norton, Goodwin, Alexander Agassiz, Bowditch, White, and Morgan. Sandys' host in America was the son of Professor Lane, while he was lecturing at Harvard, and later he stayed with Professor Norton and other friends, when he travelled to the Universities of Pennsylvania, Bryn Mawr, Columbia, Vassar, Cornell, and Johns Hopkins. Mrs Sandys did not accompany him to America but spent the Easter vacation in Italy; from his letters to her we may quote his description of his first lecture at Harvard.

In the evening Mr and Mrs Lane came out from Boston to dine with the Morgans, and I delivered my first lecture (on Petrarch and Boccaccio) to an audience of five hundred densely packed in the rising seats of the theatre, with the Deputy-President of the University and Professor Goodwin and many other professors and students and the general public present. There was a graceful speech of brief introduction by Professor Morgan in which he referred to my *Orator*, *Bacchae* and *History of Scholarship* and to my Latin Oration for the Members' Prize on Abraham Lincoln. There were loud and enthusiastic cheers at the beginning and end of the lecture, which closed exactly at one minute past nine o'clock. References to the Old Cambridge and the New were cheered, and any little touches of humour, but famous names such as those of Longfellow and Oliver Wendell Holmes were not. I was prepared for this attentive and genial kind of audience, and, indeed, if they had once begun to cheer the famous names that I mentioned, it might have added materially to the length of the lecture. The Lanes and others were full of kind congratulations at the end, and I returned with the Morgans to their house, where many of the Classical staff of the University were present.

Conditions however were not always so favourable. Writing from Cambridge, Sandys says:

I have got up a little earlier on this my last morning at Harvard to write you a few lines.

On Friday, 31st of March, I gave my Extra Lecture on the study of Greek at a meeting of the Classical Club consisting of Teachers and students of the Classics. The meeting was held and the lecture given not in the usual theatre of the Art Museum, but in the large upper room of a "Gymnasium" or Gymnastic Club, and a piano was being played in the room below during nearly the whole of the lecture! I had a very attentive audience, and, although the piano was really disconcerting, my friends (who were rather ashamed of the incident) assured me that I did not betray the slightest emotion at the interruption. I assured them that I had done many more difficult things in my day.

In the course of his lecturing tour and his visit to the Niagara Falls and Toronto, Sandys made many friends and renewed many acquaintances; foremost among these was Professor Charles Eliot Norton, on the occasion of whose death Sandys wrote a letter to *The Times*, in which he expressed his gratitude for the hospitality extended to him by Professor Norton at his home at Cambridge and at the Saturday Club at Boston.

On his return to England the Lane Lectures were published by the University Press, and they met with as warm a reception in print as they had in actual delivery. We read in *The Athenaeum*:

> Within the necessary limits of some half-dozen lectures the subject is almost ideally treated in the little volume before us. Dr Sandys combines with a profound knowledge of books a light touch and an appreciation of the spirit of place so that he knows the literary value not only of tracing the course or revival of learning, but also of recalling to his readers the physical aspects of the homes of humanism....His sketches of the Italian humanists are admirable; they are drawn with art, and strengthened, not overweighted, by the learning that inspires them.

It was this quality of lightness combined with such unique knowledge that explained the wide popularity enjoyed by both the *History of Classical Scholarship* and the Lane Lectures. The first volume of the *History of Classical Scholarship* passed into a third edition in 1921, the year before his death, and in 1915 he published an abridgement of the *History* under the title of *Classical Scholarship*. In this volume the most important developments of classical scholarship were traced with less elaboration of detail, and the subject became more accessible to those who had not a specialised knowledge. In this shorter history Sandys retained the attractiveness of his writing and did not sacrifice form to material, as is the tendency in so many text-books. A pleasant example of the style of his work is afforded by his description of perhaps the greatest of Leyden's professors:

The same love of uniformity was exemplified in the case of Attic Greek by Cobet and his immediate followers. Such a tendency may even perhaps be regarded as a national characteristic of the clear-headed and methodical scholars who dwell in a land of straight canals rather than of winding rivers, a land of level plains varied only by a fringe of sand-dunes, a land saved from devastation by dikes that restrain the free waters of the sea.

In December 1905 the sudden death of Sir Richard Jebb caused deep sorrow to Sandys. Sandys, who was three years younger than Jebb, had been closely associated with him ever since his entering the University; both of them were keenly alive to the importance of widening the circle of influence of the classics, and when Jebb took the leading part in the foundation of the Society for the Promotion of Hellenic Studies and in the establishment of the British School of Archaeology at Athens, he had the loyal support and co-operation of Sandys. Another link between them was that Sandys succeeded Jebb as Public Orator; but the most important point of agreement between them was their humanistic attitude to the classics, an attitude which transformed the function of classical studies and brought them more directly into relation with modern life. In honour to the memory of this great scholar Sandys revised and edited Jebb's translation of the *Rhetoric*, to which he added an introduction and supplementary notes and revised and re-edited Jebb's edition and translation of the *Characters* of Theophrastus in 1909.

During the years 1900–14 Sandys not only produced

his most valuable and most mature work, the *History of Classical Scholarship*, but he maintained his high rate of literary production in spite of the fact that in 1914 he reached his seventieth year. In addition to the *History*, which would have occupied the greater part of a lifetime for many scholars, he published in the course of these years an edition of Demosthenes, *Second and Third Philippics*, *De Pace* and *De Chersoneso*; he contributed chapters to the *Cambridge Companion to Greek Studies*, edited in 1905; he published the Lane Lectures in the same year; he contributed chapters on Latin Literature, from John of Salisbury to Richard of Bury, and on Scholars, Antiquaries and Bibliographers to volumes I and XII of *The Cambridge History of English Literature*, in 1907 and 1915, and articles on Pausanias, the two Plinies, Greek Law, and the History of Classical Studies to the eleventh edition of the *Encyclopaedia Britannica* in 1909; he edited the two works of Sir Richard Jebb already mentioned in 1909; he collected, revised and edited a select number of the speeches which he had delivered during the years of his Oratorship from 1876 to 1909 in a handsome volume entitled *Orationes et Epistolae Cantabrigienses*; he wrote an article on Ancient University Ceremonies, which was published in the *Fasciculus J. W. Clark dicatus*, in 1909; and in 1910 the *Companion to Latin Studies* was published under his general editorship and included several articles from his own pen. He was at the same time engaged in preparing some of his earlier works for re-edition; his editions of the *Bacchae* and the *Select Private Orations* of Demosthenes reached fourth editions in 1900 and 1910, and the first volume of the *History of Classical Scholarship* and his edition of Aristotle's *Constitution of Athens* were edited for the second time in 1906 and 1912. In addition to this Sandys performed the arduous duties of the Public Orator and carried out his University and College offices with scrupulous diligence. In 1907, under stress of work, he resigned his Lectureship at St John's College, but until the end of his life he took great interest in the business of the College, to which he was deeply attached.

In June 1907, on the occasion of the seventh Jubilee Celebrations of the foundation of Repton School, Sandys as the most distinguished of Old Reptonian scholars was requested to compose a school song in Latin; the *Carmen Repandunense*, which was warmly commended by W. Sanday as "quite admirable—I could not improve a syllable of it" and by Dr Peile, who recalled the year when he examined Sandys for the University Scholarships "when he wrote by far the best Latin Lyrics", was set to music and sung at the Celebration in the presence of the author. In it Sandys gave expression to his affection for the school, dwelling lovingly upon the scenery round Repton:

> Qua Trivona, lapsu lento
> purior fluens argento,
> castra barbarorum lambit,
> prata, silvas, colles ambit—

and in the manuscript of a speech made at an Old Reptonian dinner we read:

"In rising to speak to the toast of Floreat Repandunum, my first feeling is one of personal gratitude for all that Repton did

94

for me as a boy, gratitude for the generous aid bestowed upon me by my headmaster, Dr Pears, and my housemaster, Mr Latham, gratitude for the healthy influence of school chapel, gratitude for the careful training in accurate scholarship then mainly supplied by Mr Johnson. My next feeling is one of grateful remembrance of the friendships formed at the school, and of the pleasant days thereby spent in the home of one of my schoolfellows....The word "Repandunum" recalls some other lines in another language, lines which I wrote at school, on the old Roman camp and the long windings of our famous river:
"longis ubi flexibus errans
perque Repanduni campos Romanaque castra
explicat aeternos Trivona argentea fluctus".
While the Trent can apparently inspire boyhood and youth with some touches of poetry, I fear that in maturer years the Cam, in my own case, is only productive of prose.

Of later visits to Repton we have no records in his papers. Time had already severed many of the connections which bound him to the school and he outlived the friends of his schoolboy days: one of the most intimate of these, the Rev. W. Vale Bagshawe, Master of the Lower School at Uppingham, from 1880–1904, predeceased him by one year, and in an obituary notice Sandys refers to the Sunday walks in his company which formed one of his warmest recollections of Repton. As a loyal supporter of Dr Pears and his successors and as a prominent old Reptonian, Sandys served his school as she had served him; he was a worthy representative of one of the greatest periods of the school's history.

Sandys' reputation as a scholar, which had been so signally enhanced by the acclamation of his *History of Classical Scholarship*, and his prominence in public and University life as Public Orator, in which capacity he presented the most distinguished statesmen and scholars of the time, won him many honours during these years. Already a Litt.D. of Cambridge and Dublin Universities he was the recipient in person of an Honorary LL.D. at Edinburgh University in 1909, and the same honour was bestowed upon him by the University of Athens in 1912; and in the former year he was elected a Fellow of the British Academy. On the occasion of the Seventh Centenary of Roger Bacon, celebrated at Oxford in 1914, Sandys read a paper to the Academy concerning the life and writings of Roger Bacon, in which he defined the relation of Bacon's works to Hebrew, Arabic, Latin and Greek and discussed his service to Science; the concluding words of this erudite paper might well be applied to Sandys' own service to classical studies:

"We have seen" (he writes) "that he 'has come very near to a satisfactory theory of scientific method'. His scientific studies covered a wide range; he was interested in every one of the sciences, taken separately, but we know from his own testimony that he realized the close connexion of all the sciences with one another, and their mutual interdependence as parts of the same whole. He tells us in his *Opus Tertium* that 'all the sciences are connected, and foster one another with mutual aid. They are like parts of the same whole, every one of which accomplishes its own work, not for itself alone, but for the others also'."

He subsequently gave lectures on this subject in connection with the Modern and Medieval Languages Board in Cambridge.

In June 1911, the honour of knighthood was conferred upon Sandys in the list of Coronation Honours. This timely recognition of his services to learning and to the University evoked warm congratulations from his numerous friends both inside and outside Cambridge; it was felt to do honour not only to Sandys personally but also to the University which he had as Public Orator represented for thirty-five years. "To be a belted Knight", as C. W. Moule of Corpus Christi College wrote, "may not perhaps add greatly to the happiness of a life of fruitful learning and scholarship and thought and eloquence and travel;—yet a public recognition of excellence is always welcome, and I rejoice in your knighthood for yourself and for the University you have served so long and with so much distinction." The letter ends with a neat allusion to Sandys' position as Orator:

> Facunde Orator, seu Docte libentius audis,
> Qui iamdudum alios scis celebrare viros,
> Nunc liceat Grantae nunc et tibi gratuler ipsi,
> Quod tandem Insignis tu celebreris Eques.

The Arms adopted by Sir John Sandys were designed to suggest his connection with his College and with Lancashire, and they were inscribed in a window of the Pears Hall at Repton School dedicated to distinguished Old Reptonians and including the Arms of Sandys' friends and almost contemporaries, Professor Sanday and the Hon. Mr Justice Denman. Shortly after the coronation of King George and Queen Mary in Westminster Abbey, at which Sir John Sandys was present as a representative of the University, the Four Hundredth Anniversary of the Foundation of St John's College was celebrated and the approbation with which his speech was received bespoke the popularity which he enjoyed in the College and in the University. Nor was this popularity due solely to his scholastic achievements (for these are so pre-eminent that it is easy to overlook another and not less important side of his character); in a "portrait" of Sandys published in *The Gownsman* of October 28, 1911, stress was laid upon this less obvious trait in his character:

> Lastly, one might speak of Sir John Sandys as friend; but to do so would be to unfold memories of many years and to tell things one keeps to oneself about a great scholar's kindness to a freshman, sustained through decades of change. Let it be enough to say that those who do not know him intimately do not know him at all, and can form no idea of the attachment which the quiet kindliness, dignity and magnanimity of his character can win.

Since the termination of his Tutorship in 1900 and of his Lectureship in 1907, Sandys naturally had less opportunity of making the acquaintance of the younger members of St John's College, and, at the same time, his increasing years made it more difficult for him to become intimate with those of a younger generation. But until the end of his life he and Lady Sandys entertained many friends at St John's House, to which he moved in 1913 from Merton House, and his affection for his former pupils is manifest in the letters which have survived. Two letters written to the Rev. Charles Elsee in 1911 afford a clear insight into the kindliness of his nature and into the busy life which he was leading at this time.

5 *March* 1911.   *Merton House, Cambridge.*

My dear Elsee,

I have read your long letter with the greatest interest and I have much pleasure in sending a contribution towards clearing off the debt on your temporary church and parsonage....For the last two terms I have been in rather feeble health, possibly caused, or aggravated, by the labour of bringing out the *Companion to Latin Studies*, some of the contributors to which were exceedingly dilatory persons. I have found myself losing weight rather rapidly, but I am assured by the faculty that all my organs are sound....

For the last two terms I have been engaged in preparing a new edition of my *Constitution of Athens*, in which, happily, I have no co-operators to hamper me. I have written several short lives of dear old Mayor, which will be partly gathered up in a slightly longer life in *The Eagle* for this term.

With kind regards from Mrs Sandys, I remain, my dear Elsee,

yours affectionately

J. E. SANDYS.

30 *October* 1911.   *Merton House, Cambridge.*

My dear Elsee,

I can congratulate you on the completion of your Church Building Fund. I had heard of Sayle's visit to yourself, and I gathered that even John Mayor would have been satisfied with your exemplary manner of life.

I have recently spent a week in writing for the *Dictionary of National Biography* the lives of Mayor, and Charles Taylor, and A. S. Wilkins; I have also taken the Chair at a meeting on Prayer Book revision held in the Combination Room of St John's and addressed by the Bishop of Sodor and Man and by Dr W. H. Frere, who were in striking agreement on the subject.

The Master, as delegate of the University at the Fifth Centenary of St Andrews, received an honorary degree. While he was being presented, a slip of paper was passed along a row of visitors stating that he was "a son of the Manse of Dairsie", whereupon an Englishman unfamiliar with the phrase exclaimed: "Dear me! What strange titles these Scotch people give themselves". He assumed that the Manse of Dairsie was a title like the Marquis of Carabbas.

I send herewith a recently published portrait extracted from a large photograph taken by request in Boston, during my visit to Harvard and other American Universities....

With kindest regards I remain,
ever yours affectionately,

J. E. SANDYS.

During these years Sandys and Lady Sandys spent many of the vacations in foreign travel, visiting most often the south of France, Italy, and Switzerland; although he kept no diaries of these tours, the value of his knowledge of the Continent was manifested in his writings. When he fell ill in the summer of 1911, a visit to Caux and Interlaken sufficed to secure his recovery. The temporary failing of his health, as he suggests, was due undoubtedly to overwork. In addition to the business which he mentions in his letters, his duties as Public Orator, and his offices as a member of the Board of Classical Studies and as an Examiner, Sandys was himself contributing in 1911 to the *Companion to Latin Studies* and also delivered two papers to the Cambridge Philological Society, of which he had been President in 1890. It is typical of him that all he did was executed with absolute thoroughness; the subjects of the two papers, "The tribes of Cleisthenes and the map of Attica" and "The mechanism of the κλεψύδρα and the restoration and explanation of the text of Ἀθηναίων πολιτεία, c. 67 §§ 2, 3", were expounded with reference to geography, inscriptions and vase-paintings. The articles which he wrote for the *Companion to Latin Studies* (of which he was general editor) comprised the Geography of Italy, Latin Prose from Cato to Cassiodorus, Epigraphy, and the History of Classical Scholarship; from a review appearing in *The Antiquary* of the second edition of this work, the following extract shows the excellence both of the design of the whole and of the articles by Sandys himself:

The whole book seems redolent of fresh research, and many of the illustrations—*e.g.* the earliest known Latin inscription on metal on the gold fibula from Praeneste of the sixth century; the photograph of the noble panel from the Ara Pacis Augustae; and the curiously beautiful decorative relief of "Perseus and Andromeda" from the Capitoline Museum—demonstrate the interest and value of the new paths recently explored in Roman and Latin archaeology. It is, perhaps, to the chapters on Public and Private Antiquities and on the Arts and Epigraphy that readers of this magazine would chiefly turn for guidance and accurate information; but as Goldsmith on our cover gives us his monthly exhortation to "love everything that's old", not forgetting our friends and manners, as well as books and wine, we may warmly welcome this new companion to the studies begun in youth. The plan of the work...shows the care with which Sir John Sandys and his colleagues have mapped out the tremendous field of what the Latins, and Rome in particular, did for the progress of the human race....From the earliest period of Latin nationality until the time when, with Boethius, we stand on the threshold of the Middle Ages, the life, communal and private, of an august race is here set out in careful and methodical detail. The volume is worthy of the best traditions of the University and the Press which have issued it.

This opinion is confirmed by the following letter:

18, *Norham Gardens, Oxford.*   *July* 5, 1911.

My dear Sandys,

I have now read your paper on the Geography of Italy, and am glad to congratulate you upon it as an excellent piece of work.

I am particularly impressed by the way in which you have brought together a large amount of information without rendering it at all dull, and by the skill with which you have constantly pointed out the influence of the geographical features of the country on its history, and have illustrated them both by quotations from Latin authors. Your account of Sicily is especially interesting.

Yours sincerely

H. F. TOZER.

In 1914, before the outbreak of war, two further honours were conferred upon Sandys; he was appointed by the King of Greece a Commander in the Order of the Saviour, and he was elected a Fellow of the Royal Society of Literature. The former was especially gratifying to him as one interested not only in the study and promotion of Classical Greek but also in the history and development of modern Greece. Shortly after his election, Sandys read to the Society of Literature a paper on "The Literary Sources of Milton's Lycidas, with special reference to Certain Latin Poets of the Renaissance". It was a subject particularly suited to the training and ability of Sandys, and the wide interest it aroused was reflected by a correspondence in *The Times* and instanced by the following letter:

June 29, 1914.   *Hindleap, Forest Row, Sussex.*

Dear Sir John,

May I, after reading the report of your extraordinarily interesting discourse upon the sources used by Milton in *Lycidas*, ask you a few questions?

One is whether you have noted many passages in Milton indicating a knowledge of Dante? The paucity of such passages has struck me, but I may possibly have overlooked many observed by you....

You will (of course) print in full your lecture which is—if I may be permitted to say so—one of the most instructive contributions to poetical criticism made for a long time. I shall hope then to have the pleasure of studying it in detail.

Very truly yours

JAMES BRYCE.

In 1914 Sandys attained his seventieth year. The ill-health which had threatened him in 1911 had quickly passed away and during the years of the war he was well and active; in the robustness of body and mind, which he showed during the remainder of his life, we may see the strong determination and will-power which was so marked a trait of his character. The *History of Classical Scholarship* had set the seal of distinction upon his scholastic achievements, and the richness of the vein which he had tapped for the wider appreciation of both Latin and English Literature was proved by minor works such as the papers on Roger Bacon and the sources of Milton's *Lycidas*. Finally, in such a work as the *Companion to Latin Studies* he gave generously of the mellow experience in the many branches of classical learning, which he had accumulated during a long and fruitful apprenticeship. During the remaining years of his life he performed the arduous duties of the Public Oratorship, until he felt that the increasing number of Honorary Degrees made it impossible for him to conform to the high standard of presentation which he had set himself; but until his death, the mental energy which was so fecund in this period of his life never flagged.

CHAPTER VI

1914 1922

UNTIL the outbreak of the Great War, Sandys' seventy years of life had passed in profound peace, broken only by the Indian Mutiny, during which his elder brother was killed at Delhi, and by the South African War, in the course of which Sandys had lost some of his friends and former pupils; for fifty years, too, he had travelled on the Continent under settled conditions, and his courtesy and his interests had won him many friends in foreign countries. He was, moreover, keenly appreciative of French, German and Italian culture, and, in the more limited field of classical studies, his own enthusiasm in the pursuit of truth and the affinity of his publications to the best Continental, and especially German, work had transcended the narrowing barriers of nationalism. The cultural κοινή of Europe, which must have seemed so secure, and towards the realisation of which Sandys' work as a scholar and as Public Orator and Cambridge representative at University Celebrations on the Continent had contributed a share, was rudely shattered in 1914 and has not yet been fully restored to life under post-war conditions.

Of Sandys' attitude to the war there is no trace in his correspondence, but two of his activities indicate the liberality of his views and a freedom from the rancorous spirit, to which non-combatants inclined. He endeavoured to the best of his ability to preserve the cultural side of life free from the corrosive and temporary influences of war: thus, while his work in the University and in the study continued much in the same manner as before, his influence in the outer world was directed to the preservation of the ideals, with which and for which he had always lived.

As a Fellow of the Royal Society of Literature, Sandys was elected a member of the Committee formed by that Society in 1916 "for promoting an Intellectual Entente among the Allied and friendly countries". He attended as representative of the University of Cambridge the Special Conference held in this connection under the presidency of the President of the Board of Education, and in his address he discussed practical methods of promoting the object of the Society, referring in particular to the influence of the University Press and the Syndicate for Local Examinations and University Extension Lectures.

Secondly, he resisted the proposal made by the Government to convert the British Museum into a department of War Service, being the first to write a letter of protest and showing himself the protagonist in the subsequent negotiations. The history of this "nine days' wonder", as Sandys styled it, was published for Sandys by the University Press, and we quote therefrom the following passage in his letter to *The Times* on January 1, 1918:

In the name of scholars and archaeologists and lovers of learning and of letters throughout the land I deem it to be my duty to protest against the proposal. Like the famous Museum of Alexandria, our own Museum has long been a splendid shrine of ancient sculpture and modern learning: a treasure-house of untold wealth, whose name is to be found on almost every page of the story of recovery of the past for the knowledge of the present, and for a trust to be held for the future. It has long been the goal of eminent archaeologists of many lands, who within its walls have laid the foundations of their future fame.... It is not for me to eulogize the great services of those who in the past have made the Museum what it now is...but I do not envy the feelings of the head of a great Government Department who goes down to posterity as the Minister who did so grievous a wrong to the national treasure-house of ancient sculpture and of modern literature as to imperil its safety. It has long been the Prytaneum of our country's fame, the lode-star of the civilized world. We are the trustees of a far-off posterity, and must make sure that the treasures handed down to us are preserved for ever, not for England only, but for the world at large.

The lead given by Sandys was followed by many eminent scholars and men of public influence, and by January 9 Sandys was able to print and send copies of letters and notice of the resolutions of ten learned Societies, including the British Academy and the Classical Association, to Members of the House of Lords and of the House of Commons, before the debate upon the issue was opened. In deference to the opposition the Government decided to abandon the project. An expression of the gratitude of the Trustees was subsequently conveyed by Sir Frederic Kenyon, then Director of the British Museum, to Sir John Sandys "for his services in drawing attention to the peril in which the Museum had been placed"; and at Sandys' request, as Chairman of the Committee of the Cambridge Museum of Classical Archaeology, copies of important archaeological works published by the Trustees were presented by them to the Library of the Cambridge Museum. His good judgment and sense of proportion had carried the day.

The most important product of the later period of Sandys' writings was his *Short History of Classical Scholarship*; in this he compressed and comprised in one volume the subject-matter of his monumental work on Classical Scholarship, thus increasing its attractiveness for the general reader. Its value is well estimated in *The Educational Times* of August, 1915:

Sir John Sandys' *History of Classical Scholarship*, in three volumes, is a work well known to scholars. The present work, complete in one volume, treats the same theme within a more moderate compass, and is intended for the classical student and the general public. Scholars of primary importance are treated with almost the same fullness as before, while the work of less important men is omitted or dealt with very briefly. The book covers an immense range from the sixth century B.C. to the present day, and the achievements of men of every age and every nation who have worked in the field of classical study are recorded in this wonderful summary. The rhapsodes of early Greece, Aristarchus and the great critics of Alexandria, Thomas Aquinas, Roger Bacon, and the schoolmen of the Middle Ages, the scholars of the Renaissance, Bentley, the modern scientific critics, Lachmann, Madvig, Munro—all these and many others are here passed in review. As a work of reference this book is invaluable to every classical student, but it is also a book which may be read for pleasure and interest. One may forget for a moment the strife and bitterness of these troubled days in this record of patient labour in the cause of learning, where the feuds of nations have no place.

In the same year Sandys edited the text and translation of Pindar for the Loeb Classical Library, of whose Advisory Committee he had been a member since the inauguration of the Library. The translation, which was in prose, met with less commendation than his other works, but then no one has yet found a medium of translation worthy of the "pride" and "ample pinion"

> That the Theban eagle bear
> sailing with supreme dominion
> through the azure deep of air.

The introduction and the treatment of the text received the approbation of Professor Gildersleeve of Baltimore, the leading authority of the time on the poet. This edition passed into a second edition as early as 1919. On the Tercentenary Commemoration of Shakespeare, in 1916, Sandys contributed to the book entitled *Shakespeare's England* two chapters on Education and Scholarship, and in *A Book of Homage to Shakespeare* he wrote the delightful epigram on the Tomb of Shakespeare:

> Ἐνθάδε πατρώῳ ποταμῷ πάρα, παῦρα Λατῖνα,
> παυρότερ' Ἑλλήνων γράμματα, παῖς ἔμαθες·
> ἐνθένδ' ἀνδρωθεὶς ἔμολες ποτὶ πατρίδος αἴης
> μητρόπολιν, σκηνῆς τ' ἄθλα μέγιστ' ἔλαβες.
> ἐνταυθοῖ δ' ἄψορρος ἰών, καλὰ πολλὰ πονήσας
> εὗρες τέρμα βίου καὶ κλέος ἀθάνατον.

> Here, as a boy, beside his native stream,
> He once did learn "small Latin and less Greek";
> Hence, as a man, he the great City sought,
> To win the noblest prizes of the Stage;
> Hither, with all his work well done, he came,
> To find the end of life, and deathless fame.

He refers to this work in memory of Shakespeare in a letter to Mr Elsee, dated August 1916:

The Shakespeare Tercentenary gave me, in various respects, a somewhat busy time. As a Fellow of the British Academy, which began the organisation of the Commemoration and then left it to develop itself on independent lines, I happened to be a member of the Executive Committee, which began its labours before the war, and, after having secured the Patronage of the King, was about to proceed to approach the other crowned heads, when it became necessary to limit the proceedings to England alone. However, various dramatic performances were organised by the Theatre and the Stratford branches of the Committee, and our secretary, Professor Gollancz, organised the production of a great Book of Homage, to which some 166 persons were asked to contribute as representative of England, and of other friendly nations and in many other languages besides English. I was asked to contribute some Latin prose, but preferred the briefer task of contributing a short passage of Greek verse—of which I enclose a copy. The co-operative work, *Shakespeare's England*, published by the Clarendon Press lately, included some forty pages by myself on Education and Scholarship in the age of Elizabeth, written some five or six years ago, and published after many delays due to other contributors and partly (doubtless) to the war. I am now filling part of my spare time with the preparation of an Introduction to the study of Latin Inscriptions.

This latter work, entitled Latin Epigraphy, containing fifty illustrations, was first published in 1918, and the following extract from *The Saturday Review* is representative of the reception given to it:

An accomplished scholar, Sir John Sandys has done much of recent years for classical education. To wide erudition he adds an unusual gift for brief yet clear enunciation and illustration of facts and principles, and the present book is one of his happiest achievements. It fills an obvious gap, for it is the first introductory manual of classical Latin epigraphy to be published in England.

The demand for this book, the last published by Sandys, has been so great that a second edition was produced by

S. G. Campbell in 1927—a striking testimony to the freshness of his mind at the age of seventy-three. Before he fell ill, he published a paper entitled "Tin[commius]" in *The Numismatic Chronicle* of 1918, dealing with the restoration of the incompletely recorded name of a British king preserved in the *Monumentum Ancyranum*.

During the war Sandys and his wife spent the vacations in visits especially to Malvern, where they used to walk in the hills. There was a good Public Reading Room, for he never liked to be divorced from books or papers, and he also enjoyed the company of Mr G. M^cN. Rushforth, a former Director of the British School at Rome.

Of his family we hear little; since the death of his step-mother in 1902, to whom he was very deeply attached, he had lost the only one of his brothers still alive, the Rev. Joseph Samuel Sandys, who died in 1906 through heart-failure; with his step-brother and two step-sisters he kept in touch until the end, and they were beneficiaries under his Will. In Cambridge itself he had many friends and maintained his regular habit of taking walks into the country in their company.

As Public Orator he still had many duties to perform, and the conditions of war-time often demanded new methods of presentation. He describes such a situation in a birthday letter of 1917 addressed to Mr Elsee:

I spent part of this anniversary in presenting two for the Honorary Degree of M.A. whose work for Cambridge lies nearer to Leeds than the public services of the American Ambassador and of Scipio Africanus Minor do to England, in the geographical sense of that term. I have seldom had to deal with subjects which, at first sight, seemed so intractable as the Mayor of the newly-created county-borough of Darlington, who is "one of the leading stockbrokers in the North of England, and is the University Extension Secretary for the County of Durham, and President of the 'Local Centres Union' which consists of the Extension Secretaries in all parts of England". However the stockbroker was transformed into a "votary of Mercury", the Secretary into a *dextera*, and the President into a *caput*; and similarly in the case of the other recipient, the "Local Centre" became a *castellum* and an *arx media* among the *propugnacula* of our University.

With the end of the war came a flood of Honorary Degrees. As Sandys always made a point of researching into the careers of each recipient and touching upon matters of distinction, in the course of the oration, he found the duties of presentation particularly arduous: on December 26, 1919, he accordingly wrote to the Vice-Chancellor resigning the office of Public Orator. In the following letter addressed to Mr H. W. Simpkinson, who came into residence at St John's College in 1872 and formed, as we have mentioned, a life-long friendship with Sandys, the reasons which actuated him to resign the Oratorship are clearly expressed.

4 *January* 1920.   *St John's House, Grange Road, Cambridge.*

My dear Simpkinson,

Lady Sandys and I were glad to receive, with your good wishes, such a fairly satisfactory account of yourselves during the past year. It was only during the Easter Vacation that we had a good holiday at Malvern, leaving Cambridge as early as possible in the Vacation so as to reach West Malvern in time to avoid a threatened strike....

The Easter Term was marred to a large extent by the fact that the Council of the Senate proposed Graces for conferring honorary degrees on more than thirty generals and admirals etc in recognition of their services in the recent war, but, while the authorities of Oxford wisely were content with a comparatively small batch of carefully selected war-heroes, almost all of whom were presented for their degrees by the end of June, it was not until the latter part of July that after a short holiday at Letchworth I was able to present a group of eleven, with nine others at two different dates in the Michaelmas Term.

The vacancy in the office of Chancellor involved my writing an official Latin letter to Mr Balfour formally apprising him of his election, and afterwards addressing him in a Latin speech at his own residence on the occasion of his inauguration. I was thoroughly interested in both of these compositions, which gave me a good reason for reading Alderson's admirable life of our Chancellor; and, in the course of one of them, I referred to the fact that no civilian had ever received louder and more prolonged applause in my time in the Senate House than Mr Balfour when he received his honorary degree thirty-one years previously at the time of his great success as Secretary for Ireland.

August was spent in Cambridge, while I was completing the distribution of the books and papers of the late Mr J. B. Mullinger, as his residuary legatee,...September was also spent in Cambridge, as we felt certain that we should fare less well elsewhere than at home.

The Michaelmas Term, which involved me in seventeen pieces of official work as Orator, in the way of either speeches or letters, kept me so constantly employed that I hardly had any time for my personal correspondence or my private affairs. There was also every prospect of a laborious Easter Term with further honorary degrees, and the great incursion of a Medical Congress, as soon as it was over, to be probably followed by a visit of Pan-Anglican Bishops before the end of July, both of these involving heavy work in the so-called "vacation". Hence you will hardly be surprised that I found myself compelled to consider seriously the question of resigning the office of Orator, which I had held for an unprecedented number of years. It had been impracticable to resign during the war, so I seized the opportunity to finish four books which were published in due course. It was still less possible to vacate office during the vacancy in the Chancellorship. I had therefore to make up my mind to resign at the first and, to all appearances, the only convenient opportunity, when, as it happened, I was exempt (for this January) from the duty of examining for the University Scholarships.

I have not forgotten the help that I received from you and yours in the Long Vacation of 1876, which ended in my election to the office which I have been proud to hold for so many years, with the consciousness of being fully equal to its difficult demands until of late the burden began to threaten to be too severe for my present powers. I enclose a cutting from a local paper which will give you an intelligent young Scotsman's account of part of my career, inspired to some extent by a personal interview.

My immediate plans during the present term are to see through the press a third edition of the *Companion to Latin Studies*, and then to begin a third edition of the first volume of my *History of Classical Scholarship*, and to get such time as I can for general reading. For the Easter Vacation Lady Sandys is planning for us a visit to France including Gallo-Roman cities in the South and other places in the West between Toulouse and the Pyrenees.

At Pau, in the latter region, we have lately lost our friend, Mr W. F. Smith,...

I cannot close this rather dry and precise record of a laborious year without sending to you and yours our best wishes for the New Year. I know that this letter ought to reach you on the anniversary of your birthday. Many happy returns! I remember you every day of my life.

Yours affectionately
J. E. SANDYS.

In an official letter to the then Vice-Chancellor, the Master of Emmanuel, announcing his resignation, he ends with the words:

While I now resign that office with sincere regret, I hope to continue to serve the University as a member of the Committee of the Museum of Classical Archaeology. I also hope, with a renewed sense of leisure, to resume such literary labours as are appropriate to my present age, and thus to return, in the evening of life, to "the quiet and still air of delightful studies".

Sandys was now in his seventy-sixth year; he received by Grace of the Senate the title of *Orator Emeritus*, and on May 19, 1920, the seventy-sixth anniversary of his birthday, he received the titular degree of LL.D. *honoris causa* in recognition of his services which had extended over forty-three years—a period of office considerably exceeding that of any of his predecessors. It was a source of great satisfaction to him that he was succeeded in the Oratorship by the present Orator, T. R. Glover, a former pupil and a close friend: we quote from the speech made by Mr Glover upon presenting Sandys for the degree of LL.D., in which he refers to the services to the University and to the personal kindness of the *Orator Emeritus*:

Adest ipso natali die qui hoc in loco ut Epistolas Academicas recitaret, ut viros laudatos Academiae praesentaret, plus quam septingenties adstitit, qui post tres et quadraginta annos rude donatus ad studia illa reversus est quae semper amavit. Demosthenem, Euripidem, Isocratem, Ciceronem exposuit, Aristotelis *Rempublicam* sarcophagis Aegyptiis erutam edidit, immo senectutis in limine fontis Pindarici haustus non ille expalluit. Rem etiam maiorem aggressus est, et omnem Eruditionis Classicae Historiam ausus est

tribus explicare libris
Doctis, Juppiter, et laboriosis.

Sed labores sibi non lectori imposuit, et immensi illi doctrinae thesauri cum voluptate perleguntur. Si discipulo talia licet confiteri, ex quo primum Collegio nostro interfui, hunc semper mihi comem recordor, semper iucundum, semper amicum fuisse.

On June 23 of the same year the Honorary Degree of Litt.D. was conferred upon Sandys by the University of Oxford. He stayed on that occasion with Sir Herbert and Lady Warren, to whom he presented a copy of the *Orationes et Epistolae Cantabrigienses* (1909-19), which formed a companion to the earlier volume covering the period 1876-1909; on receiving the present, Sir Herbert Warren wrote: "I think you do rightly by yourself in retiring, and you have certainly earned the right to do so. Yet I cannot witness your resignation without keen regret, and a sense of the end of a unique chapter full of long and distinguished achievement".

Free at last from the claims of University business, Sandys turned all his energies to his literary work, for several of his earlier works awaited re-edition and he was always anxious to keep abreast with his general reading. But the evening of life drew in quickly. After making a tour in southern France—his first visit to the Continent since the outbreak of war—he returned to Cambridge, and suffered from a severe attack of influenza in November 1920. He appeared to have fully recovered, but the illness had affected his heart. In the following spring during a tour in the Pyrenees he felt unwell and suffered from shortness of breath; at St Jean de Luz he was informed by a doctor that his heart was weak. On his return to England he was forced to live the life of an invalid. But despite the condition of his health he continued to work and read and write; he had never spared himself and he continued to follow the interests that were so dear to him. The following letter— the last that we have from Sandys to Mr Simpkinson— is expressive of his energy and industry.

My dear Simpkinson,

We were glad to hear of the early prospect of your son's marriage, and of his call to Trinidad. You will be sorry to lose him, but England has good reason to be proud of her Colonies, and to be grateful to all who will help to promote their prosperity.

We remember with pleasure our visit to Lucca many years ago, and have been recalling it while reading Eustace's *Classical Tour in Italy*. During the last Easter Vacation we had a very satisfactory tour in Southern and Southwestern France, including places already well known to us, namely Nîmes, and Arles, and Avignon, and many that were new to us, such as St Remy, Carcassonne, Cahors, Rocamadour, Limoges, and Bourges. Since then we have seldom been staying away from Cambridge, but, early in this Long Vacation, we spent two or three weeks in the refreshing air of Letchworth Hall Hotel.

The honorary degree conferred on me at Cambridge on May 19 (the anniversary of my birthday) was followed by a degree at Oxford where we were the guests of my friend Sir Herbert and Lady Warren.

Meanwhile, I have finished the revision of the *Companion to Latin Studies* and the first volume of my *History of Classical Scholarship*, in both cases for third editions, which will be published in due course. The interest I have shown in Petrarch in the sequel to that volume has prompted Canon E. H. R. Tatham to seek my support in his proposed publication of an extensive work on *Petrarch and his Times* which he has long been preparing. His letter has only reached me during the last few days, when I am little able to do anything more than is absolutely necessary.

On Tuesday, November 9th, soon after the arrival of your letter, Arthur Gray was my guest at the Fellowship election dinner; on Wednesday, I walked a long way to a lecture by Mrs Arthur Strong; and on Thursday evening, I suddenly had a feverish attack, which has kept me in bed ever since. At present it is quite uncertain how soon I shall resume my ordinary life, but the doctor has for the first time found it unnecessary to visit me to-day, and has left me some time (though but little strength) to write to my old friend, whom I daily remember.

With our kindest regards and best wishes to yourselves,

I remain ever yours affectionately

J. E. SANDYS.

P.S. I am just finishing W. H. Mallock's *Memoirs*, and have recently begun reading aloud Mrs G. M. Trevelyan's *Short History of Italy*.

Throughout 1921 he lived the life of an invalid, and remained in Cambridge except for a visit to Folkestone; of this year too we read in a letter to Mr Elsee:

I have lately been reading a number of the books bequeathed to me by Dr Mullinger, the most interesting of which have been J. Cotter Morison's *Life of St Bernard*, William Bright's Lectures on the early history of the English Church (with much on St Cuthbert), and J. B. Mozley's *Historical and Theological Essays*, including a good deal of vigorous writing on Stratford and Laud and Cromwell and Dr Arnold, who is far more highly praised as a headmaster than as a theologian.

It was a source of disappointment to him that he was unable to take part in the meeting of the Classical Association held in the summer of 1921 in Cambridge, and his health was so weak on the return from Folkestone that he "found it necessary to dictate letters resigning his chairmanship of the Museum of Classical Archaeology and various other duties".

In the following spring he had so far recovered as to pay a visit of over a month's duration to Mentone in the company of Lady Sandys, and on his return even attended a meeting of the Classical Board. For the summer Lady Sandys had arranged a stay in Switzerland, a country which he loved. But on July 6, 1922, while passing through the third court of St John's College on his way to the Senate House to be present at the conferring of an honorary degree on the Duke of York, he stopped to talk to a friend and suddenly fell down. The end had come painlessly; he was wearing the scarlet robes of the Doctor of Letters, the emblem of his services to learning, and he died in the grounds of the College, to which he had devoted fifty-five years of life. The circumstances of his death formed a fitting culmination to a career of service to the University. In the words of Dr Pearce on his resignation of the office of Vice-Chancellor:

The University has to mourn the loss of some who have served her well in their day and generation. On July 6 at the very moment when the ceremony for the conferring of honorary degrees was about to commence, our Orator Emeritus, Sir John Edwin Sandys, died suddenly on his way to the ceremony, *felix opportunitate mortis*.

CHAPTER VII

In Memoriam

A FEW words remain to be said *in memoriam.* We have discussed elsewhere the determination and the kindliness of a character moulded under the influences of a Christian home and strengthened by the example of missionary life, zealous in the pursuit of truth, reserved in emotion, capable of strong and abiding friendship; deeply imbued with religious feeling, unflinching in the execution of duty, direct in the conduct of life. From such qualities of character emanated the influences exerted by his own life upon the lives of others, and they were influences of such value as to survive his death. Of his contribution to scholarship we have already spoken in detail; the most distinguished and the most valuable of his individual works was undoubtedly the *History of Classical Scholarship*, but his services to classical learning must also be measured by his edition of the *Bacchae*, his work on Greek and Roman oratory and his *Companion to Latin Studies*.

The motto which Sandys was fond of quoting, "By learning, you will teach: by teaching, you will learn", truly describes Sandys' development as a scholar, from the days when he was a pupil of the great coach Richard Shilleto to the latter years of his life when his most valuable work was produced. The remarkable accuracy and solidity of Sandys' work and the prodigious power of memory with which he was endowed

owed much to that early training; writing of Shilleto's influence on Sandys, J. S. Reid emphasised this debt:

> It may be said, I think, that the most vital lesson which a young scholar can have imparted to him is the knowledge, which may become almost an instinct, of "quid nequeat, quid possit oriri" in the field of scholarship. This acquisition Shilleto could and did most certainly convey. His training made it almost impossible for a young man to start hotfoot immediately after his degree on some wild goose chase in the field of learning. The happy hunting-ground of the irresponsible youth of to-day, the dim borderland between history and fable, had not come within the ken of the classical student.

But Shilleto's training was open to the charge of narrowness, and it was the peculiar merit of Sandys himself that he had the vision to enlarge the range of classical studies; for, while he shares the description "A Scholar of the Renaissance" with J. E. B. Mayor, his claims are greater in that he added to a purely literary interest an enthusiasm for the artistic and archaeological aspects of classical learning. Of this wider interest the *Bacchae* was the first indication, and it was followed by other works of more specialised value, such as the *Introduction to Latin Epigraphy*. Incidentally this last work may be cited as an example of Sandys' adaptability, for he only studied the subject in the first instance, because one of the contributors to the *Companion to Latin Studies* had failed him. Of equal importance was his influence upon contemporary scholars as an active member of the Committee for the foundation of the British School of Archaeology in Athens and as Chairman of the Museum of Classical Archaeology. His *History of Classical*

Scholarship and his lesser works, such as the paper on the Sources of Lycidas, mark another and particularly humanistic facet of Sandys' talent; for by bringing classics into closer relation with the history of modern Europe and with the literature of England in particular he laid open to the general public and to the student a new field of fruitful study. In these two aspects of Sandys' work we may see his most abiding contribution to classical scholarship. At the same time his name will for long be connected with books of wide learning, such as the *History of Classical Scholarship*, the *Dictionary of Classical Mythology* and the *Cambridge Companion to Latin Studies*. Both in the quality and in the originality of his work, Sandys merits a distinguished place among Cambridge scholars.

As Public Orator, Sandys was endowed with one valuable asset; his editions of Greek and Latin orators and rhetoricians had bred in him a real faith in the power and artistry of Rhetoric, which combined with the gravity of his bearing and the dignity of his manner to lend weight and precision to his oratory. His voice, however, was rather soft and lacked the silver cadence which marked the oratory of Sir Richard Jebb; the difference was noticeable when Jebb delivered speeches in the place of Sandys on the occasion of the latter's indisposition (about 1905) or absence on holiday. In his own words Sandys gave his rules for Oratory as follows:

As to how to make a speech the matter can be compressed into a nutshell. Firstly

"Never be prolix".

Secondly, and these maxims I cannot claim as my own, for they originated with Martin Luther,

> "Stand up firmly.
> Open your mouth boldly.
> Leave off timely".

I have always acted on these rules and, as a consequence, have never had the mortification of feeling I was addressing an unfriendly audience.

Sandys took the utmost care not only in the preparation of the text of his speeches but also in the preparation for their delivery. "To the conscientious labour bestowed on the duties of his office as Orator I can testify," wrote J. S. Reid, "for he had the habit during many years of coming to consult me about the speeches before they were delivered." In the method of presentation Sandys introduced an innovation: previously the Orator spoke from the centre of the Senate House, but he took up his position on the dais, the better to command the attention of his audience, while the recipient stood below the dais.

We have already spoken of the Latinity of his speeches and the skilful manner in which he recorded the salient features in the careers of the recipients; an opportunity of comparison with the work of orators in many other Universities is afforded by the published congratulatory addresses to the University of Aberdeen on the occasion of the Quatercentenary in 1906. The record of his forty-three years of service in this office is contained in the two volumes of *Orationes et Epistolae Cantabrigienses*, forming in themselves an excellent presentment of brief biographies of practically all the eminent men of his he was succeeded in this venerable office by his former pupil, Mr Glover, and that the reformed pronunciation, which he had done so much to introduce, remained in use.

During his lifetime Sandys had amassed a splendid library. By the generosity of Lady Sandys and in accordance with Sir John's wishes, 1467 volumes from this library were added to the library of the Museum of Classical Archaeology; the present excellence of that library owes much to Sandys not only for this gift of books but also for his services on the Managing Committee for almost fifty years. We quote the following extract from the Eleventh Annual Report of the Committee from *The Cambridge University Reporter*:

By the death of Sir John Sandys on 6 July 1922 the Museum has lost one of its most distinguished and effective supporters. He had acted as Chairman of the Committee continuously from 1911, the year in which the Museum was first separately administered, to October 1921, when he was obliged by failing health to resign office. Throughout this period of transition and expansion Sir John Sandys' judgment, energy, and tact were of the utmost value to the Department. The successful inauguration of the Library Fund and the Casts Fund, in 1913, was mainly due to him. Moreover, repeated gifts of books, pamphlets, and periodicals attested the special interest that he took in the Library of the Museum.

Shortly before his death Sir John Sandys presented to the Library 84 volumes of archaeological works, including many magnificent folios, together with a collection of classical photographs and facsimiles. Further, the Museum has received from Lady Sandys no fewer than 1467 volumes (chosen by the Reader in Classical Archaeology) from the library of Sir John Sandys. This munificent gift comprises not only works of an archaeological or historical character, but also numerous classical Texts, Commentaries, Monographs, and Dictionaries. It thus fills a gap in the Museum Library, which now contains a total of nearly 9000 volumes.

Sandys was also much interested in the St John's College Library and had for many years constantly attended the Library Committee meetings; in his Will he bequeathed a small legacy to that library, and, in accordance with his wish, more than 1000 books were transferred to the College Library after his decease. Sir John's Coat of Arms is inscribed in one of the western windows in St John's College Library, together with those of other College Benefactors. The house, called St John's House, which Sir John and Lady Sandys had built on College property in Grange Road, was bequeathed to St John's College; Lady Sandys was entitled to retain it during her lifetime but she has not done so. In memory of his services to the College, a brass plate has been erected in the St John's College Chapel with the inscription:

IN PIAM MEMORIAM
JOHANNIS EDWINI SANDYS EQ
QUI DIU SOCIUS DIU TUTOR POSTREMO BENEFACTOR
COLLEGIUM ERUDITIONE ILLUSTRAVIT
ET LATINITATIS ORATOR PURISSIMAE
STUDIORUM ANTIQUORUM HISTORIAM CONSCRIPSIT
GRATO ANIMO POSUERUNT AMICI
MDCCCXLIV–MCMXXII.

In his Will, Sir John Sandys further left stock to the value of two hundred pounds a year for the foundation of the Sandys Studentship in the University of Cambridge. The holder of the Studentship

is required to devote himself to study or research, according to a course proposed by himself and approved by the Electors, provided that such course may in special cases be altered or varied with the consent of the Electors. He is also required to spend a large part of the year at a foreign University or other place of learning (to be approved for this purpose by the Electors) such as the British School at Athens or Rome.

By the generosity of Lady Sandys, to whom under the terms of the Will the income of the said stock was to be paid during her life, the first election to the Sandys Studentship was made in 1929. The conditions required of the holder bespeak the wish of Sir John Edwin Sandys that to others should be extended the opportunity to cultivate the interests which had brought him happiness in life, the interests of scholarship and of travel.